EMBRACING MY
Sexy Sixties!

20 INSPIRATIONAL STORIES FROM PHENOMENAL, CONFIDENT & BEAUTIFUL WOMEN

VISIONARY AUTHOR SHARON J. BULLOCK

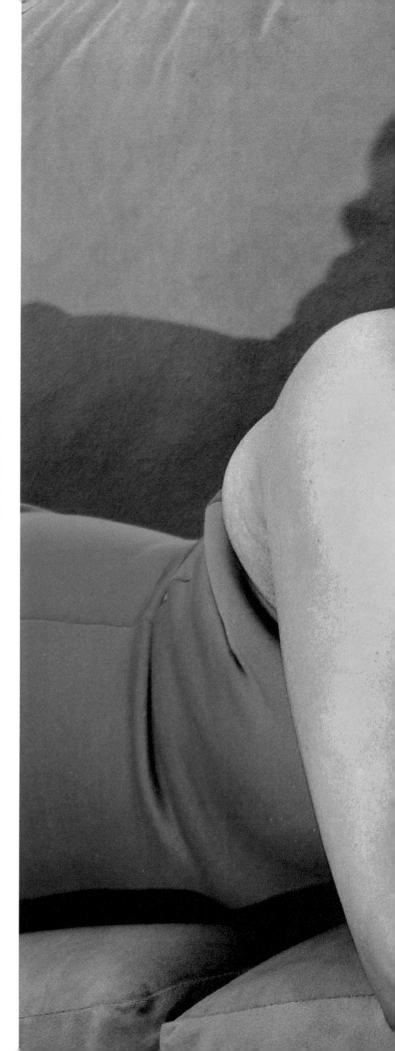

Published by:
Sharon J. Bullock
www.embracingmysexysixties.com
Washington, District of Columbia

Book Design
Giovanni Misagrande
Inspired by Dr. Tasheka L. Green
www.2eseasons.com

Editing
Desiree' H. Bonner
DHBonner Virtual Solutions, LLC
www.dhbonner.net

Laura Dorsey
Editor & Content Advisor

Dr. Natasha Pollard
FYJ Consulting, LLC

Library of Congress Control Number: 2020923220

ISBN FOR HARDBACK PRINT: 978-1-7351286-0-3
ISBN FOR PAPERBACK PRINT: 978-1-7351286-2-7
ISBN FOR eBOOK: 978-1-7351286-1-0

Printed in the United States of America

CONTENTS

DEDICATION

To my former late husband, James L. Bullock, Jr. — Thank you for being my biggest cheerleader and always believing in me. You were the wind beneath my wings.

To my dearest college best friend, the late Cherie' Harp Roberts — You were just shy of your 60th birthday when heaven received another angel. I will forever miss you, my friend.

To my PHENOMENAL Favorite Aunt, the late Faye Burruss. You were the biggest influence in my life's career and business path into the Beauty & Fashion industry. You were my Shero!

To my AMAZING parents, Willie D. & Viola Jackson — I am so grateful and so blessed to still have you in my life! You have molded me into the woman I have become. Your guidance and wisdom will be with me forever. I love you both for life & beyond!

FOREWORD

*S*exy and Sixty! Two words that don't normally go together. Yet, some have done it and can teach others to do the same.

Sharon Bullock is one of them!

She is the epitome of sexy and sixty! She is a master at teaching women how to dress to impress and how to think in ways that create interest from the opposite sex, whether it is a husband or a significant other.

Here are a few words to express why we're drawn to someone who is "sexy and over sixty."
Alluring.
Captivating.
Charming.
Clever.
Enticing.
Fascinating.
Graceful.
In Control.
Intriguing.
Mysterious.
Ravishing.
Smart.
Subtle.
Stunning.
Wise.
Witty.

If you want to move in her direction…read this book. If you want to get closer to discovering what she's all about…read this book! The manner of how she presents herself has *a distinctive appeal to men*!

You might have tough times—Sharon certainly has—but she has decided to not allow herself to look like what she has been through.

We've watched Sharon build her inner strength by having "character building" experiences forced upon her. Plus, she has peppered her life with dogged determination and resilience. Yet her gentility, humility, determination, and resilience are steadfast.

Dee and I celebrate Sharon and the other Sexy Sixties women who are showing the world how to celebrate life!

~ Dr. Willie Jolley and Dee Taylor-Jolley

ENDORSEMENTS

"Embracing My Sexy Sixties will have you inspired to live your best life at any age! It is encouraging, empowering, and exciting all in one! The women's messages are enlightening and have you yearning for more. It is a must read!"

~ Melanie Bonita, #1 Amazon Best Selling Author of "Daily Dose of Declarations!"

"Sharon, you have always been a style trendsetter. Thank you for offering us such a positive, uplifting, and empowering gift. This book will surely uplift our sisterhood to celebrate life. The stories inside will help your readers to shine in their worthiness without apology, excuses, or shame."

~ Jewel Diamond Taylor, aka The Self-Esteem Dr.

"Once, entering into the age of your 60's was considered the threshold of when a person approaches the last mega phase of production in their life. It's a new day! Women in their 60s now are in a state of "Thrive hold", birthed out of experiences from tragedy to triumph from all areas of their lives. Sharon, thank you, my fellow sexy, sixty sister for shining a spotlight on our seasoned, sassy, saucy, and sexy stories of the Bold, Beauty and Brilliance of women in their sixties."

~Linda Clemons, Global Expert, Sales and Nonverbal Communications

"This book is perfect for women of any age to embrace, whether they have or have not entered the decade of their sixties! The stories and beautiful pictures will keep you engaged and wanting more as you read through this inspirational and very impressive coffee table book. Sharon, I have known you for over thirty years, and I am so proud of you! I love the mix of women from all backgrounds, shapes and sizes. I love their strength and perseverance, and how many of them have come to love themselves. If you're a woman in your sixties or will be when the next one comes out, I urge you to share your stories — the good, the bad and the ugly, so that you might lift up another sister who might see themselves in you!"

~ Germaine Bolds-Leftridge, CEO - GBL Sales, Inc.,
CCO - Ubiquitous Women's Expo

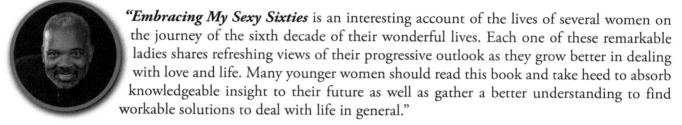

"Embracing My Sexy Sixties is an interesting account of the lives of several women on the journey of the sixth decade of their wonderful lives. Each one of these remarkable ladies shares refreshing views of their progressive outlook as they grow better in dealing with love and life. Many younger women should read this book and take heed to absorb knowledgeable insight to their future as well as gather a better understanding to find workable solutions to deal with life in general."

~ Rodney Wayne Branche, Publisher/Editor-in-Chief,
Copa Style Magazine, @copastylemag

"Wow! Sharon's book, *Embracing My Sexy Sixties* is a wonderful tribute to womanhood at any age. This book is a generous offering of inspirational stories that breathe with hope, laughter, engagement, and strength! It's an exciting journey taken by a mix of women from varied backgrounds and life experiences. Sharon, nailed it with this one!

No matter what age you may be enjoying now as a woman, there will always be some woman coming behind you who will look to you for guidance and there will always be some woman ahead of you who can offer you wisdom. You know your story better than anyone else. Tell it, share it!"

~ Louise Robinson, President, "Sweet Honey and The Rock, Inc"

"Embracing My Sexy Sixties explores beauty and wisdom in a creative, collective way never seen before! All of these women are now my role models as they have given me a roadmap to becoming sexy at 60!"

~ Jacqueline Thompson, Owner, Overdue Recognition Art Gallery

"Over the years, a combination of market demands of beauty products and services has created a supply of women who do not want to fit culture expectations of how aging should look and what defines 'normal'.

Here in this book you will see that these women do not fit the norm. In fact, they destroy the narrative that you have to appear like the aging, hopeless, dependent woman of yesteryears. You will read and understand that everything that you have gone through in life is about who you are and who you are becoming. You will learn how they used their experiences to create new ones. Simply by exploring activities to take care of their soul, mind and body. All in all, the biggest lesson you will take away is to love and embrace all of you."

~ Charlene E. Day, Communication Strategist

"*Women — embracing their sixties*! The ladies' stories in this wonderful book introduce us to women in their sixties at turning points in their lives. In doing so, in the face of becoming sixty, I enjoyed these story collections immensely. The stories offer intimate views of women turning sixty in a way that makes the reader almost voyeuristic. I am watching these women live and love, and it is fascinating to do. The ladies, loving and living— I found to be the greatest gift you could give the reader. This is that rare collection of stories that I will definitely read again and probably more than twice.

~ Russell Price, King Of Marketing, BE THERE Magazine

ACKNOWLEDGMENTS

Special Thanks to the following whom, without your help, advice, encouragement, input, and/or services, this book would not have been possible...

Cover Photo & (most) Interior Photos - Bill Hart Photography
Roy Cox Photography (Pamela Reeves & Coniece Washington)
Jeffery Rice, Jr. (Laura Dorsey)
Greg Blakley, Fritzphotographics.com (Maeion Bryant)
Leslie Hendricks, Visual Effects (Rosetta Thompson)
Don Baker Photography Group & Debra Clanton (Betty Entzminger)
Jackie Hicks - jhicks1-fondmemories.com (Miriam D. Martin, MD)
Robert Garrett (edits)
Louis Bryant Photography (edits)
Cover Photo Makeup - Sade Dennis
Maeion Bryant, Pro Makeup Artist - Maeion Beauty & Co.
Donna Holley-Beasley - Faces by Donna
Sandra Libby - Caldwell Banker Brokerage, Annapolis, MD
Turf Valley Resort - Nicole Motsay
Dr. Tasheka L. Green - To Everything There Is A Season
Wendy Thompson - DC Spotlight
Elena Design Studio
Sisters 4 Sisters Network, Inc.
George M. Kent
Laura Dorsey
Dr. Natasha Pollard
Dr. Hattie Washington
Florence Champagne
Brenda B. Chavis
Jackie Thompson
Melanie Bonita
Charlene Day
Kimberly Paul
Toy James

We are NOT our
Mothers' Sixties...

INTRODUCTION

*B*eing in our sixties now would have probably been the time to sit down, relax, maybe travel a little, and enjoy the rest of our lives in retirement, as our Mothers would have. *But we're **NOT** our mothers' Sixties!* We have lived, loved, laughed, cried, succeeded, failed, gotten back up again, and we're still here! Whether we have married, divorced, been widowed, or single, we have raised our children, started our businesses, advanced in our careers, or just started over. Now is the time to tell our stories! We are the new 40s and 50s, just born a little sooner. Our lives are just beginning. We're starting over — in more ways than one.

I never knew what to expect when entering my sixties. I used to say, "When I start to grow old, I'm going to fight aging every step of the way!" When I got here, I thought, 'I don't "feel" any older, except for a few extra aches and maybe a few forgetful "senior" moments.' So, what does being sixty-ish look and feel like? I've been told that I don't look my age, and certainly don't act any differently. When I looked around me, I was in awe at my beautiful sisters in their sixties who have inspired me. I wanted to highlight Phenomenal women in this age group to give others approaching this milestone something to look forward to and to be proud of. I wanted to collaborate with them to tell their stories in this full color, coffee table book that could be passed on for generations to come. It is our time to shine! The idea of this Anthology book started with a few simple questions:

- Are you in your sixties, but everyone thinks you look much younger?
- Are you dynamic, successful, and living your passion?
- Do you have a story to tell that will inspire, motivate, and encourage other women?
- Do you have health and beauty secrets that are keeping you healthy and looking younger?

With these questions in mind, I invited an array of amazing women to be a part of this project.

Some of us are starting new relationships after being widowed, divorced, or just starting over. I, for one, have lost everything: My dream home, my business, my best friend, and eventually, my husband. I had to

make a choice — either be swallowed up in a deep dark depression from a whirlwind of losses or decide to live the rest of my life to the fullest. I have chosen the latter.

Why did I add the word "sexy" to the sixties? A lot of people would say that 'sexy' is about the body. But not me . . . I think that "sexy" is a woman with confidence and power. Power is about loving yourself and having strength from within. So, even if you are not wearing a sexy outfit (that I put together), you still feel sexy. This book is written to encourage, inspire, and give women approaching, or already in this age group, something to look forward to. We are starting new careers, new businesses, finding love for the first, second, or third time, and enjoying life! We have made our mistakes and accomplishments and have learned from them all.

Some of you will be astonished when I say that living never seemed so magnificent as it does now. In these pages, you will meet some Phenomenal, Confident and Beautiful Women in their Sixties, who will inspire you to be whatever you want to be, do whatever you want to do (legally), requiring permission from no one but yourself. Sexy Sixties is a state of mind, and that state of mind comes in all shapes and sizes.

It is unique for every individual. You'll meet a doctor, a lawyer, speakers and writers, teachers and entrepreneurs, community leaders, sales executives and clergy, actors, singers, and models, all with one thing in common:

We're Embracing Our Sexy Sixties!

Pamela Reaves, 63

ACKNOWLEDGING, EMBRACING, AND UNLEASHING THE POWER OF MY SIXTIES

Pamela Reaves

There is a blessing bestowed upon women during their passage from youth to maturity. With maturity comes a certain allure, grace, dignity, and power that has withstood the test of time. This remarkable metamorphosis has been achieved through experience that isn't always pleasant, comfortable, or attractive. However, the results are astounding — and in retrospect, the mature woman knows that the zenith of her maturity doesn't happen despite unpleasant, uncomfortable, or unattractive experiences inherent to living life, but rather because of them.

I liken the timeline of women to the formation of the diamond, which starts as a carbon. Through a vigorous process, wherein a chemical composition is formed through intense heat and pressure, the diamond ultimately becomes a brilliant crystallized stone that is said to be unique and a miracle of time. Just as the diamond is precious with inimitable value as the result of intense heat and pressure, the mature woman is one of the Creator's most beautiful, effervescent, and fascinating creations, who is also a miracle of time. Having experienced my own intense heat and pressure throughout my journey, I can state, without reservation, that I am that beautiful, effervescent, and fascinating creation known as the mature woman.

I am incredibly proud to be counted among that special group of women who have decided to operate from a position of power, defining their sixth decade in accordance with their own terms, conditions, and standards. It is our moxie, which differentiates us in ways that are not only unique individually, but also collectively. We neither desire nor need to define our sixties as the new thirties or forties; those definitions belong to those amazing groups of women. We've already been there, done that, and possess a treasure trove of advice, nuggets, and priceless wisdom to offer the group of women following our path.

Acknowledging the impending passage to maturity prepared me for the transformation. In a world that places a premium on youth, it's not always easy to recognize the blessing of aging gracefully. However, by acknowledging the inevitability of aging, I decided to define my fifties, sixties, seventies — and the years beyond — on my terms. I am not stereotypical in anything and decided that conventional wisdom, as it relates to aging, would not define me. I took the helm and began preparing myself mentally, spiritually, and physically for the transformation that was going to take place, whether I wanted it or not. I found that when I acknowledged the milestones before me, the expectation that something different (foreseen and unforeseen) was going to occur, saved me from giving in to fear and the urge to fight the inevitable. I was not going to allow an obsession with youth to rob me of embracing my supreme value, living my life accordingly, and unleashing my inner power to ensure that the rest of my life is the very best part of my life.

There is no proverbial fountain of youth, clock to turn back the hands of time, or any other age reversal remedy to include in our maturation plans. From personal experience, I've learned that staying relevant, vibrant, and sensual at any age is a choice. My choices have served me well, and now I'm in that wonderful space where my sage advice, lifestyle, and personal wellness programs are invaluable, not only to me, but for others as well. There is no shortage of inquiries from other women and men of all ages who want to know how I've maintained my beauty, exuberance, and zest for life. They seek my counsel on how to attain and preserve the conquering spirit of an experienced woman who now commands attention without demanding it. These complimentary inquiries are not limited to my physical appearance because the enlightened person understands that the type of beauty that never fades extends far beyond appearance.

The woman who embraces her sixties belongs to an exceptional group of women who also embrace change. She knows that change is inevitable, constant, comes with opportunity, and is necessary. . . and that lessons, well-learned, bring [added value, development, and clarity regarding life's cycle. My lessons have always had their origin in my decisions. All decisions either reward or penalize us. I found that these rewards and penalties came in the form of triumphs or tragedies, gains or losses, advancements or setbacks, joys or sorrows, connections or disconnections. By embracing change, I became an ever-evolving woman – that evolution means I will never be permanently placed in any position, whether it be in my favor or not.

With this knowledge, it became clear to me that those experiences of my youth, which I viewed as overwhelming, heartbreaking, or obstacles, wound up being blessings in disguise. With these changes, the Creator, in His infinite wisdom, prepares us for the remarkable level of courage, confidence, and flexibility needed to enjoy an enriched life by the time we reach the sixtieth anniversary of our sunrise (birth).

Now that I'm in my sixties, it may be that I'm paying closer attention to my age group, but it seems like every day I read about, hear about, and meet other women in their sixties who are awesomely interesting in some way. Their conversations, among other things, are stimulating, sad, helpful, heartbreaking, funny, inspiring, and provocative. A woman who has been living for six decades can engage in conversations about everything with the voice of experience; you will not hear the quiver of uncertainty in her voice. After engaging in a conversation with her, you will not walk away wondering if she knows what she's talking about. You will, however, walk away in amazement, wondering how she seemed to know what you were talking about, while you were struggling to explain yourself.

When the mature woman walks into a room, she walks in like royalty, although she has been humbled by a myriad of life's experiences that weren't always in her favor. When she acknowledges, embraces, and unleashes her power, those in the room not only see her when she makes her entrance, they feel her. They may or may not be able to articulate what they are feeling and seeing, but they know there is something magnetic, commanding, and mysteriously persuasive about her. No matter what her physical height is, she appears as a giant in whatever space she occupies.

I am eternally grateful for the lives of the women before me whose journeys were like blueprints. Like them, I have grown, learned from my past experiences, and became pliable when it comes to change. I now know when to exercise restraint and when to exercise my power. My posture of confidence emanates from the knowledge that, while my humbling experiences may have at times caused me to bend, they were unsuccessful in breaking me. At this stage in my life, I acknowledge and understand that I am not exempt from heartache, but I know the validity of that age-old adage, "And this, too, shall pass." This experiential knowledge has blessed me with the confidence to walk with my head held high, even amid adversity. While my younger contemporaries may be screaming, crying, and swearing that life for them is over whenever confronted with the tumult that is certain to visit all of us before our sunset arrives, experience has taught me that life's challenges, obstacles, or disappointments are not the end of the world.

When I was a younger woman, it wasn't uncommon for me to witness how mature women could sit among those who were younger and hold court, while their subjects hung on to every word they spoke. In my innocence, I recognized, valued, and embraced their wise counsel. Using them as points of reference, I knew that I was going to be the type of queen who moved with confidence and authority. I was committed to self-development with the goal of becoming the type of woman who is comfortable in her skin, not concerned about fidgeting around every couple of seconds to adjust something (e.g., her hair, clothing, makeup) that isn't perfect. My definition of perfection was changing. I was no longer overly concerned with whether my hair was perfectly coifed.

Comfortable in my skin also meant being comfortable with my sensuality. For me, the sexy sixty-something woman knows that part of her allure may be a head of tousled hair after her husband or lover suddenly grabs her to share a soul-stirring kiss just before she leaves the house. This woman's confidence will not allow her to worry over something as inconsequential as a button missing from her blouse. She just makes sure that her adjustment is such that the missing button winds up at the perfect place, rather than a vulgar place. She is not worried that her lipstick may be a little smudged while eating out at a restaurant. She is more concerned that she and her date enjoy their food and each other's company. Being a sexy sixty-something woman, I now celebrate my imperfections as my sexy messes, and they are some of my most captivating features.

Sexy doesn't have to be one dimensional. I find attributes such as *intelligence* sexy and discovered that the wisdom I've gained over my lifetime is like a sedative; the things that used to make me anxious, cause angst, arouse anger or instill fear no longer move me. I've developed a calming, relaxing, soothing, and quieting spirit that younger women tell me they aspire to possess. Now that I'm in my sixties, I have earned the honor of being a point of reference and the evidence that a whole lot of living is attainable at any age. I've lived long enough, gone through enough, and prevailed over enough to recognize this sedative I speak of as the supernatural peace of God that surpasses natural understanding.

I am a living, breathing, walking, talking body of evidence that sixty-plus is an extraordinary space and place to be in. The road that I've traveled to arrive in my current place and space has not been without fiery trial and tribulation. Just like the diamond, the fire did not burn me — it refined me. In all honesty, I'm wired in such a way that I usually choose the rough road, so I've had more than my share of bumps, bruises, and mishaps. There have been plenty of times when I've had to self-admonish, telling myself to get somewhere and take a seat, to pull back, stop doing so much, or take the path of least resistance, but that's not who I am.

I've had more than what I thought was my share of disappointments when hopes and dreams were not coming to fruition soon enough. I've always been an ambitious woman and while working in a corporate environment I have experienced disparate treatment, not being adequately valued for my contributions, and dealing with the stresses inherent to the African American female in that workspace. Thank God that as a young woman, I decided not to marinate too much on those things intended to work against me, but instead, turned them into leverage. As I matured, I became a master at counteracting adverse conditions with courage and confidence. Through professional development, I learned that, although I couldn't control what people thought about me or change their stereotypical thinking, if they were resolute concerning their biases, I could control my response.

This acquired mastery didn't go unnoticed by those with whom I've worked over the years in diverse corporate cultures. Over the last forty-plus years, I've earned the respect of professionals across the board, from entry-level through senior management. My confidence is displayed in every aspect of my corporate life, earning me the reputation of being a consummate professional. My courage is appreciated, and I am viewed as fearless. There have been occasions when I have been surprised at how others perceived me in my corporate life, like the time during my sixtieth birthday party when a colleague from the early years got up to share her testimony about our working relationship. She spoke about how I had motivated her, the things she had learned from me, then the surprise came when she said, "Pam feared no man." There was so much passion in her voice that I could feel the impact of my fearlessness in her professional life. It was an honor to hear, years later, that I had instilled courage in another woman in the workplace.

The sixty-something woman who knows her value no longer depends on the assessment of others when it comes to evaluation. Everything that I've been through has taught me something and contributed to the woman I've become. I'm confident in my knowledge, experience, and contributions to the bottom line of others. After enjoying years of progressive experiences and opportunities, I concluded that it was time to use my gifts and talents to create my own company. By taking purpose-driven action, I was able to achieve several accomplishments after the age of fifty. I became a Certified Professional Coach, a national public speaker (as of June 2020, an international speaker), a published author, a brand ambassador for business owners in the fashion industry, and developed a line of skincare products. I've learned to congratulate myself on my accomplishments and feel no compelling reason to wait for the applause of others.

"The truth sometimes hurts, but it always heals." ©

I know too well the heartbreak of the dissolution of relationships that, at the time, I wanted to last for a lifetime. I've always been considered a beautiful woman, but have had my moments when I questioned my physical appearance. When we are young and naïve, there are certain dynamics at work, in relationships that are not in our best interest, that will have the most beautiful woman in the world questioning herself. In our youth, we haven't lived long enough to know that the criticisms are usually grounded in the other party's insecurities, so in order to keep the beautiful woman in her place, the other party will find ways to influence her to call into question her beauty.

As I've matured and become well-acquainted with my physical features, state of health (mentally and physically), spirituality, and sexuality, the opinions of others may be noted. Still, their opinions aren't necessarily my truth. As a woman in her sixties who is embracing my God-given magnificence, I know the difference between constructive and destructive criticism and decide to either accept criticism or reject it. I was raised by a woman whose physical beauty was the manifestation of her internal beauty. As much as I enjoy making up and dressing up, I continuously work on inner beauty. If I am feeling beautiful, my vocabulary and conversation are beautiful, my behavior is beautiful, and I maintain a beautiful spirit. All that emanates from within will radiate on the outside. While I appreciate and never take compliments for granted, I want people to experience my internal beauty; to make the connection – what they see on the outside is the inside brought to physical form.

Prior to reaching my sixties, I started to grasp a new reality that this part of life was going to be amazing and that I would be charged with passing along something meaningful to the lives of young women. I was well into my fifties when another friend invited me to a party to celebrate her milestone. The day after the party, she shared with me a conversation she had with her goddaughter. She started the conversation by asking me not to be offended by what she was about to share. She then repeated her goddaughter's question about me. This young woman asked, "Who is that woman I'm going to look like in about thirty years?" My response was, "Are you kidding me? You can't buy that type of compliment."

It was at that moment that I came to realize how our beauty can last forever. Here was someone at least thirty years my junior who saw a woman who influenced her to look over decades into her future and decide how she desires to look. During her observation throughout the evening, I'm sure she went beyond my physical appearance and saw mannerisms, heard conversations, and detected an aura that she decided to use as a point of reference. Hopefully, she will be a future point of reference; another younger woman will view her life over the next thirty years, and the cycle will continue.

As a coach, I teach three fundamental steps to how you can achieve a desired result in anything. Whoever you want to be, whatever you want to accomplish, acquire, or master, it is necessary to:

1. Acknowledge
2. Embrace, and
3. Unleash it.

This formula is perfect for the woman who has arrived, is dwelling in, or about to exit her sexy sixties. *Acknowledge it*. Otherwise, it doesn't exist. *Embrace it*. Wrap your head and your heart around your supreme value. Your vitality, sexuality, intelligence, and spirituality won't leave you if you don't abandon them. *Unleash it*. Don't hold back on anything you desire to have, do, or achieve.

I have a relative whose creed is "Live Out Loud". Don't move about quietly through this marvelous part of the voyage. Make bold statements in all that you endeavor. Refuse to be timid with your style. Step out into the world, unapologetically, in your brand worthy style, and you'll leave them with an indelible impression.

Pam Reaves is the Founder of NELLA, LLC. She is a Certified Professional Coach, Published Author, Motivational Speaker, and Entrepreneur. NELLA, LLC is the umbrella under which she operates her power coaching practice, facilitates empowerment seminars, speaks at conferences, promotes her books, and creates and distributes her skincare products.

Pam holds a Bachelor of Science Degree in Business Management; has received certification from New York University's School of Real Estate, Johns Hopkins School of Real Estate; and has completed extensive seminar training at the Practicing Law Institute in New York City. She has also received Management Training Certification from Dale Carnegie Institute. Pam has more than 40 years of progressive experience working and thriving in diverse corporate cultures in the areas of human resources, labor relations, finance, legal, and real estate. She has worked for several major corporations listed on the New York Stock Exchange and has worked directly with some of the most highly regarded Wall Street senior executives.

Pam has appeared on several radio talk shows and participated in numerous blog-radio talk shows. She has shared her expertise as a relationship columnist with readers of several online publications. Pam is the recipient of an impressive list of awards for her accomplishments and philanthropy. Her first book has been used as a teaching tool by Ray of Hope Kenya. Pam has also been a featured author and speaker at a host of other cultural events, book festivals, and expos. As a mature woman, she has been honored to represent other businesses with her image as: "The Face of Rosebud – 2014"; and "The Trendy 4U Woman". In 2015, Pam introduced her natural skincare line of products called "Essentially Good."

Pam has been married to Reginald Scriber, Sr. for over 30 years.

Coniece Washington, 67

MY VOICE, MY SONG, MY LIFE

Coniece Washington

When I was asked to participate in this anthology project book, I immediately thought, '! 'Hell, yeah!' I am age sixty-seven, I still have a lot of living to do, and I want to share my life's adventure with everyone. Those adventures in life have been sometimes good, sometimes bad, and sometimes nothing special. But through it all, I'm still here.

Glide Magazine wrote that *Shades of Shirley Horn* was, for me, a lifelong dream of sorts. The review also said that I grew up with Horn and other female jazz vocalists like Sarah Vaughn, Ella Fitzgerald, Nancy Wilson, Billy Holiday, and Carmen McRae as my main influences. I am not going to say that they were lying, but that was only half the truth. Actually, the first time I heard Shirley Horn sing, I fell in love with her groove and elegance. Due to my military service, I never had the opportunity to attend one of her shows, but I always have carried her in my heart. But let me be perfectly clear, despite my love affair with music, my first love is my family. My daughter, Shannon P. Washington-Haynes, is a smart, beautiful, talented black woman who is a beast in the creative, advertising world. Married to the love of her life, Greg Haynes, she is the epitome of "Black Girls Rock"! But I am getting ahead of myself. I was always told to never start a story at the end, so let's go back to the beginning to when this story starts. My delight at being able to participate in this project is that it allows me to tell my story, as only I can tell it.

TRENTON MAKES! THE WORLD TAKES!

I should have known that I was destined to be a singer. On April 7, 1953, in Trenton, N.J., John Pete Washington and Kate Francis Vereen Washington gave birth to a baby girl they named Coniece Washington. I share my birthday with Jazz/Blues vocalist Billie Holiday. We were a large family, and I was the oldest of eleven children: My deceased brothers and sisters - Rose Washington Glover, Darlene Washington, Renee Washington, and Tyrone Washington; and my living sisters and brothers: Paulette Washington White, Denise Washington Keys, Jerry Washington, Rodney Washington, bonus sisters - Nicki Washington, Wanda

Washington, and Deidra Washington; Uncles Willie and James (Sunny Boy) Vereen, my Aunt Bertha Brown, and my maternal grandparents, Jerry and Pauline Vereen, who are now with the ancestors.

Growing up in Trenton during the 1950s and 1960s, our family did not have air conditioning, and in the summer, my grandfather came to our home and took all of his grandchildren for a ride to cool off. As a child, I was always amazed at the iconic **Trenton Makes! The World Takes!** sign. Grandfather told the story that some Trenton area residents are certain that the coined phrase 'Trenton Makes. The World Takes' is symbolic of the goods produced by Trenton factories, which are distributed around the world. In 1910, the Trenton Chamber of Commerce put out a contest to create the slogan to be put on the bridge. The sign lit up the sky as we drove over the Delaware River via the bridge into Pennsylvania. Trenton, New Jersey, still maintains some of its colonial charm. The city is the state capital and is the namesake of William Trent, one of its leading landowners. We loved going to the Trenton Farmers Market, Cadwalader Park, and Hetzel Field Park.

I had a vivid imagination and always dreamed I would be a singer, dancer, or a nurse. My parents did not have money for lessons or interest in the arts, so I was never able to take formal lessons until I was older and could pay for vocal lessons, which I still take today. My uncle, an ex-marine and former ballet dancer, encouraged me to reach for the stars. My father was not interested in the arts, but he liked to hear me sing. As a young teen on Saturday mornings, we would watch Hercules on television, trade comic books, and eat tangerines. One day, his good friend, who was also my play uncle, came over during our time together. My father said, "My baby can sing. Sing, baby, sing!" I was never shy. Always the sassy one — fearless, with a lot of mouth — which sometimes got me into trouble. I had no problem belting out a song. God gives each of us special gifts and talents; we will lose them if we do not use them.

I love all genres of music, but Black Music is a way of life for me. The music gave me a sense of pride and helped me to become the woman I am today. As the oldest of eleven children, I remember dancing on the large front porch to James Brown's *Say It Loud, I'm Black and I'm Proud*. The pride was on our faces as we celebrated in song (the first time for many of us) our blackness. I am a child of the seventies, which, in my opinion, had the best music. The music of Nina Simone, also known as *The Civil Rights Diva* and *The High Priestess of Soul,* and songs such as *Black Is the Color of My True Love's Hair* and *Four Women* was the music my parents played in the house. Songs by Miles Davis, Nancy Wilson, Millie Jackson, Gladys Knight, Marvin Gaye were also part of the playlist at the time, as was the music on the show 'Soul Train'. I graduated from High School in 1971. Nina Simone's *To Be Young, Gifted and Black* became my theme song. The song gave me pride as a young Black, large, afro-wearing Queen! The joy I felt in my bones while dancing to Sly and the Family Stone's song *Dance to the Music* was mesmerizing. The serious way I thought about the state of Black America and my future while listening to the music of John Coltrane, Betty Carter, and Abbey Lincoln was to play an impression on my life. Jazz and Gospel Music touches my heart because they also capture the journey of my life.

MY LIFE IS AN ADVENTURE!

Like the gospel song, *Rough Side of The Mountain,* written by Mr. F.C. Barnes, life is an adventure filled with highs, lows, and joy. I moved out of my parents' home at age eighteen. I attended the local community college while working in the evening as a janitor at the New Jersey Board of Education. A child of the ghetto, education was important to me, so I could give myself a better life. I graduated from college, served in the U.S. Army, earned a black belt in karate, became a single mother, got married, divorced and suffered a loss due to the deaths of my maternal grandparents, mother, father, favorite uncles, aunt, three sisters, one brother, and two best friends.

In the military, I participated in talent shows. While assigned to Germany, I embraced living in Europe and wanted to see everything. I was single with no children then, and I became good platonic friends with a gentleman in Germany. He assisted me in performing R & B at several German clubs and private parties. Once I returned to the United States, I started singing Gospel and Jazz. I found out I was not very good at singing jazz, so I began to take jazz vocal lessons to learn and grow as a jazz artist. As a trained vocalist, I became a member of the Washington Performing Arts Society Men & Women of the Gospel Choir. In 2018, I was awarded the Montgomery County Employee's Black History Show contract. Being a single mother was difficult, so once my daughter graduated from Howard University, I told myself that it was time to do my thing! On January 31, 2019, I retired from the Government as the manager of a Mental Health Vocational Program – no more working fourteen hours per day due to consistent staff shortages!

It was my turn now.

I had started singing in my grandmother's church during my formative years, and it was time to take my love affair with music to another level. As a veteran of the United States Army, I had toured Europe and the United States, singing in various night clubs. Now I was honing my skills, performing around the Washington, D.C. area and at a variety of clubs; such as Bethesda Blues & Jazz Supper Club, Twins Jazz, The Carlyle Club, The Other Barn, Mr. Henry's, The Georgetown Ritz Carlton, The Henley Park Hotel, Café Agape, Blues Alley, and Westminster Presbyterian Church Friday Night Jazz. I have also performed at the following festivals: The D.C. Jazz Festival, The Rehoboth Beach Jazz Festival, the Mid-Atlantic Jazz Festival, and the Annual Preservation of Jazz Festival. My debut CD, *Love Changes*, allowed me to win over audiences.

MY LOVE AFFAIR WITH MUSIC

Now, as a full-time working jazz artist, my new CD, *Shades of Shirley Horn,* made two jazz charts and is played in Europe, as well as the States. I recorded all of the songs on my CD, *Shadesof Shirley Horn*, which I released in 2019. *Shades of Shirley Horn* is a collection of twelve songs that will either remind audiences of Horn's style and abilities or serve as an introduction to her. Each track symbolizes the joy of life, cherishing each moment of living and loving the experiences that come with it, whether they result in love lost or the deepening feelings of love. Fans of jazz have heard the name, Shirley Horn. However, for you reading my story, I need to introduce her to you in writing. I need for you to see how amazing she was so that you can, then, understand my desire to promote her legacy:

Shirley Horn kept a relatively low profile and was at least semi-retired in the 1970s, but continued to perform in her local area, Washington DC, until a year before her death. But even a decided lack of touring could not dim the legend of Horn. Her unique phrasing, her lack of vibrato, while maintaining a lush quality, plus her ability to accompany herself on the piano while she sang, all added to the allure of her style. As if Horn's music could not speak for itself, she was publicly lauded by Miles Davis in the 1950s. This *endorsement* of sorts allowed Horn to make a more prominent name for herself. It was Horn's *Embers and Ashes* album that caught the famed trumpeter's attention.

Horn was described by producer and arranger Quincy Jones as "like clothing, as she seduces you with her voice." Before Horn was a professional musician, she was a child prodigy who first studied classical music at Howard University at age 12. She switched to jazz after graduating with a degree in classical music. Shirley Horn can be quoted as saying, "I want you to feel what I feel. I want you to see the picture I'm trying to paint. I want you to be beside me. Be inside me. That's the way I feel."

Horn's trio recordings emerged with numerous Grammy Award nominations including one for her most popular album to date, *You Won't Forget Me*, which featured cameos by Miles Davis and harmonica player Toots Thielemans. A memorable performance in Paris yielded yet another well-received Verve release in 1992: *I Love You Paris*. That was also the year Shirley fulfilled a long-held ambition to work with celebrated arranger and composer Johnny Mandel. Their album together, *Here's to Life* hit number one on the Billboard charts for a record-breaking 17 weeks.

There could have been far more to Horn's story, but the performer passed away in 2005. My work on *Shades of Shirley Horn* CD helps to tell Horn's story and keep her legacy alive. The self-produced CD has sold very well and debuted on the Roots Music Report's Top 30, Top 50 Jazz Album Charts, and the North American College & Community Chart. *Shades of Shirley Horn* has received outstanding reviews from Midwest Records, Jersey Jazz, Jazz Weekly, Take Effect Reviews, Glide Magazine, In a Blue Mood, Audiophile Review, Jazz2Love, Bebop Spoken Here [U.K.], The Jazz Page, and Cadence Magazine. I attribute the success of the CD to the joy I receive from honoring Shirley Horn and loving her music. The press has written that my voice has the classic feel that Horn was known for.

In addition, the phrasing that highlights the clever wordplay of the lyrics is found in my rendition of Horn's songs.

My philosophical approach to my music builds intimacy with my audience. Additional reviews reflect the thought that with a voice, which is like Horn's, but unique enough to solidify her own sound, which is controlled, and no note is forced. My voice is comfortable in high or low registers. I do a great job of preserving the purity of Horn's material, staying faithful rather than trying to reinterpret. That is why audiences that listen to Horn's original and my version render an appreciation for both. With my training, there is a classic jazz feel that is established from the first note, and audiences are immediately interested in how I will bring Horn's style to life in song. When I sing, my audience is instantly aware that they are listening to tribute music. All of this success is not in a vacuum. I have an amazing band with me as I perform, and they are equally supportive. My band includes Thad Wilson on trumpet, Carl Carrington on flute, David B. Cole on guitar, Vince Evans on piano, Wes Biles on bass, J.C. Jefferson, Jr. on drums, and Kevin Kojo Prince on percussion. The program usually includes "Here's *to Life*," "*The Island*," "*Love Is Here to Stay*," "*Fever*," "*Dindi*," "*A Time for Love*," and "*I Just Found Out About Love*."

Don't get me wrong . . . my life has not always been a bed of roses. My supporters have said that I regally show the sensitive nature and vulnerabilities of being a woman. My musical delivery demonstrates to my audience the pride of being a woman; that same pride that came from growing up in Trenton, being proud of my Black heritage. At times it has been rough, but as I grew as a person, embraced my faith, and learned from my mistakes, I can truly say that I am happy with this journey called 'Life'. I read a poem called "The Dash" by Linda Ellis, which is about living life and living for today. 'Live Your Dash' is an inspirational reminder that it's not about the number of years we spend on this earth because between the date of your birth and your death is a 'Dash'. What does your 'Dash' say? It's about how we live those years that truly matters. It means to boldly live a life that impassions you while positively impacting your family, friends, community, and even strangers.

Your 'Dash' need not be perfect. It's an ongoing journey to living a life filled with you and intention, and it looks different to everyone. I want people to say "that vocalist, composer, producer, Coniece Washington, sings from her heart, captivating audiences with her incomparable, distinctive, sultry, sweet stylings." Over the course of my ascending career, I have uniquely reinterpreted standards while honoring the legacy of the vocalists who have influenced and inspired me, such as the likes of Sarah Vaughn, Ella Fitzgerald, Nancy Wilson, Shirley Horn, Billie Holiday and Carmen McRae.

Sometimes I have to pray really hard, but prayer works, and then there are times when I have to simply stand still. But I am not done with this life. My goal is to present the Great American Song Book with authenticity and integrity. My motto is *Life is an Adventure! Sometimes good, sometimes bad, and sometimes nothing special.* But I'm still here!

Vocalist, composer, producer, Coniece Washington, sings from her heart, captivating audiences with her incomparable, distinctive, sultry, sweet styling. Over the course of her ascending career she has uniquely reinterpreted standards while honoring the legacy of the vocalists who influence and inspire her: Sarah Vaughn, Ella Fitzgerald, Nancy Wilson, Shirley Horn, Billie Holiday and Carmen McRae.

This Trenton New Jersey native's love for music was developed and nurtured from an early age at her grandmother's church. Her vocal talent and pure passion for music were deepened and refined while serving in the US Army. Then, Coniece accepted various invitations and opportunities to perform in night clubs and venues throughout the United States and Europe. A trained vocalist, Coniece is a former member of the renowned Washington Performing Arts Society's Men and Women of the Gospel Choir. She has performed throughout the Washington DC Metropolitan area at venues including: Bethesda Blues & Jazz Supper Club, Twins Jazz, The Carlyle Club, The Other Barn, Mr. Henry's, The Georgetown Ritz Carlton, The Henley Park Hotel, Café Agape, Westminster Presbyterian Church Friday Night Jazz, the historic Blues Alley; and at the following festivals: The DC Jazz Festival, The Rehoboth Beach Jazz Festival, the Mid Atlantic Jazz Festival and the Annul Preservation of Jazz Festival. Coniece composed the holiday song, "Snow Covered Stars", and she self-produced her new CD, Shades of Shirley Horn, released March 17, 2019, and debuted on both the Roots Music Report's Top 30 and Top 50 Jazz Album Charts and the North American College & Community Chart. Shades of Shirley Horn has received outstanding reviews from Midwest Records, Jersey Jazz, Jazz Weekly, Take Effect Reviews, Glide Magazine, In a Blue Mood, Audiophile Review, Jazz2Love, Bebop Spoken Here [UK], The Jazz Page, and Cadence Magazine. For more information please go to her website at www.coniecewashington.com.

Dr. Cynthia S. Brown, 64

A LEGACY
OF LIFE LESSONS

Dr. Cynthia S. Brown

Life is a continuous learning experience, like waves washing ashore, bringing some things with its constant ebb and flow, picking up and dropping valuable lessons along the way. Some of these lessons come from experience, yet there are others that we learn by watching other people, television, movies, or reading books. For more than sixty years, I have relied on the advice, guidance, and wisdom of one significant person - my mother. She taught me many valuable lessons that have endured throughout my life, giving me the courage to step beyond the boundaries and expectations that sometimes I, and others, set for myself, which changed the trajectory of my life's journey.

I grew up in rural Spotsylvania, Virginia, the tenth of eleven children in a working-class family. My seven older sisters, two older brothers, and one younger brother never lived at home at the same time. We were far enough apart in ages that at no point did all eleven of us live under the same roof. In fact, my oldest two siblings were married when I was just a little girl. My mother and two oldest sisters were pregnant at the same time. My oldest niece, who happens to be my mother's oldest grandchild, is only three weeks younger than me. As a result of my large family, I have nieces and nephews who are nearly the same age as me.

My parents' marriage was unstable, causing them to separate early in my life, but never divorced. My father died when I was thirteen. So, I was primarily raised by a single mother who instilled in me the importance of being self-reliant and independent. As such, I became even more determined and driven to have a successful journey in life. I wanted to overcome the hardships and struggles that I witnessed my mother going through.

Mom was my hero. She worked hard to provide for my youngest brother and me, cleaning other peoples' homes and relying on her income to make ends meet. She was an amazing woman and the person who influenced me the most; there wasn't anything that she couldn't do or accomplish in my eyes. Not only was she my mother, but she was also my father. From changing a flat tire to building an addition

to the house, my mother taught me that there is nothing you can't accomplish if you put your mind to it. She did not want any of her children to let boundaries or obstacles become permanent barriers that get in the way of success. Her strength, faith, and sheer will to always provide the best were awe-inspiring.

When I was eight years old, my mother decided that I was finally old enough to fry a chicken all by myself. It was a pivotal moment in my life because it gave me a greater sense of independence and self-sufficiency. In my mother's opinion, frying a chicken was one of the more challenging recipes in terms of the degree of difficulty. It was not the same as fixing a bowl of Cheerios and milk. There would be daunting elements for a child to handle, like an open flame, hot grease, fire, and sharp knives. Yet, my mother was determined that I could do it, which made me determined as well. More than any other experience I'd encountered up to that point, the preparation of this dish meant that I could do a complex and challenging task, independently well. Having spent lots of time in the kitchen cooking with my mother, I learned many critical skills while fixing delicious meals; however, the confidence and success I experienced, along with her support and encouragement, motivated me to embrace future life lessons and challenges with courage.

What has stuck with me for my entire life, from that experience, was a series of lessons about facing tough situations in a careful manner. It is crucial to take your time and have patience because the best things in life are worth the wait. I learned that I could perform complex tasks just as well as I could simple ones; proper planning and preparation are necessary to tackle a challenging job without fear, but with courage and confidence. The result may not be perfect or ideal, but you can take pride in yourself for trying and not giving up.

Mom enjoyed poetry, and it was probably from her literary interest that I became so fascinated with books. I learned to read when I was three years old, and reading became my favorite pastime; it opened my eyes and mind to a world far beyond the walls of my house and the local community — spending time with books fed my desire to become more than a high school graduate, a store clerk, manual laborer, wife, or mother. The characters and their lives offered a glimpse into situations and places that were far more sophisticated and intriguing than what I was accustomed to.

My commitment to lifelong learning and the value of education was entrenched in my spirit and enriched by my mother and teachers. I loved going to school, and I loved learning. I benefitted from following in my older sisters' footsteps. They were known for their intellectual abilities, and the teachers would compare me with them. Fortunately, I was also a bright student and decided to carve out my own path instead of following theirs. My biggest goal in life was to go to college so that one day, I could become a teacher. I considered it an honor and a privilege to have the opportunity to attend college. Shifting my identity to become a first-generation college graduate was one of my proudest accomplishments; it was a break in my family history of actions and thoughts about lifestyle choices. I wanted something different, and sometimes, you must do differently in order to be different. I didn't view myself as being better than anyone else... just different. I am grateful for my mother's support and encouragement. Although she had little formal education, she desired much more for me. She nourished my love of learning and remained my forever teacher.

I'm an eternal optimist. Not because I had an astounding childhood, or that life was a bowl of cherries or problem-free, but because I chose to look on the bright side and embrace the positive. Life is about making choices — and deciding to have an optimistic attitude about my future set the stage for the remainder of my adulthood. Being a "Debbie Downer" or a negative person was never appealing; I've always been a 'glass is half-full' kind of girl, and the ability to look beyond my challenges helped with my self-image.

During adolescence, I physically outgrew most of my peers. I was the big or tall girl in practically every group. My feet were noticeable for a teen, and I stood several inches above my mother and sisters. Whenever we took a group photo, it was obvious which person was me. Adults and children always assume I am the oldest, especially when I stand next to two of my older sisters, who are each four feet and eleven inches. The good news was that it was not possible for me to wear my older sisters' 'hand-me-downs' or shoes.

Consequently, I was thrilled to receive a new pair of shoes on a frequent basis. To this day, I have a shoe fetish, and I enjoy shopping for shoes. I even own a wall plaque that says, "I can deal with anything if I have the right shoes." Shopping for back to school clothes was a perennial highlight for me. It was so much fun to go to the store, try on everything, and find the perfect outfit. Armed with confidence, determination, and a sense of fashion and style — all gifts from my mother — I began to feel comfortable with my physical stature. My mother assured me that my large frame was stately and nothing to be embarrassed about. She encouraged me to be myself and not be ashamed because I was different. It wasn't always easy. Of course, there were some drawbacks, and at times it could be confusing, but for the most part, I tried not to allow my bigger-than-average size to depress me or lower my self-esteem. The dilemma with being so tall and curvy as an adolescent was that I could be mistaken for a much more mature young woman. My physical growth and appearance made me look older than my age and created a certain awkwardness. My mother cautioned me about older boys and men who may try to flirt with me, those who wouldn't care that I was technically still a child.

As a baby boomer, I lived through several social movements, including segregation, integration, and the Civil Rights movement. I attended a consolidated, segregated school that contained elementary through secondary grade levels. Schools in my community racially integrated during seventh grade and were fully integrated by ninth grade when I attended junior high. Racial conflict reared its ugly head and pitted groups of people against one another. At times it was scary, but eventually, the fear and anger dissipated, and degrees of civility emerged. Not unlike other parents, my mother worried and prayed that everything would work out during this challenging period. The reality was, she had lived through much darker times and survived. Her advice was to focus on the positive in situations like this, as much as possible, and to surround myself with like-minded people. I worked hard as a student, registered for advanced placement classes, and excelled academically. The day finally arrived for me to graduate high school, and at that moment in time, it was my greatest accomplishment in life.

When I left home for college, I encountered a whole new world of experiences, and this was the pivotal stage that I met my college friends. It was during this time that I made friends with the people who grew up with me, as we all became adults. Our closeness created bonds that became stronger over the years as we shared life lessons and milestones. There is a friendship quote that says, "Friends are the Family We Choose." Indeed,

strong friendships are one of the most important things that people have in their life. My two closest college friends and I have a shared history that strengthens our connection and continues to sustain our love, respect, appreciation, and support for one another. In my opinion, our lives are considerably richer and more fun because of our friendships. Maintaining our friendships is an investment that we embrace and celebrate.

After graduating from college, I pursued my dream job of teaching in an elementary school. I'll never forget the day I received the call from the placement office, informing me about a position vacancy. I went for the interview, was selected and hired for the position. Continuing my education was a major part of my professional growth and development goal. Initially, I had intended to get my master's degree immediately after finishing my bachelor's degree. However, two significant life changes occurred, and it was at this point that the plan took a detour. In my mid-twenties, I became a wife, and three years later, a mother. A few years passed before I returned to school for my graduate degree.

It was necessary to adjust my personal goals and priorities to focus on my new responsibilities. Marriage changes your life in ways that can't even be fully explained or imagined; it changes who you are, the person you're with, your relationship with them, and everything else. For almost forty years, my marriage has continually evolved to adjust to both the happiest and unhappiest stages of married life. The second most significant life change occurred with motherhood. Becoming a parent and a third-generation family is a tremendous experience, and the birth of my son, Christopher, became the most profound event of my life. Anyone who knows me knows that my proudest and most blessed role is being Christopher's mother. His birthday remains one of the happiest days of the year, and I couldn't ask for a more loving, caring, and generous son. My time as a mother has brought so much joy to my life, and I look forward to another generation being added to our family in the future. Then, my status as a grandmother will become a reality.

Life is full of surprises and can shift directions in the blink of an eye. In the summer of 1987, a monumental transition occurred. We moved from my hometown, the place where I'd spent the bulk of my existence. Of course, I viewed the move as a positive. The relocation was a chance to see a different part of the world. Although the distance was not extremely far away, it still involved travel, which is one of my greatest passions; in the years since, I've been to at least thirty-six countries around the world on four continents. Growing up, I never traveled out of the country; or went on a costly trip or extravagant vacation, but my mother took us on plenty of field trips and road trips. Traveling to New York City, Philadelphia, and Washington, D.C., to see the sights was both enlightening and enjoyable. Encountering different places and people exposed us to a world much bigger than our own and fed my wanderlust. Moving to a new area provided new experiences, adventures, and opportunities. I received a considerable increase in pay, made new friends, explored the community and surrounding neighborhoods, and expanded my horizons by facing new challenges. Who knows how different my life would have been if we had we remained in Fredericksburg and never moved to Northern Virginia.

I remained in the field of education, and over time, my various teaching roles branched into administration. My intrinsic passion for teaching and love for children motivated me to enter this noble profession many years ago, a decision I will never regret. It was a privilege and an honor to be a part of so many children's lives and to make a difference by influencing the future of the world. The pursuit of lifelong learning kept me hyper-focused in an educational work environment that provided challenging, engaging, and relevant opportunities for personal and professional growth. I encountered the transformation of pedagogical practices, standards, and curriculum content. Technology, in its many forms, became the biggest game-changer in the schoolhouse.

When I turned fifty, I reminded myself that I was ten years behind schedule in obtaining a terminal degree. It was my original intent to get a Bachelor's in my twenties, a Master's in my thirties, and a Doctorate in my forties. The timeline shifted considerably, but I was determined to get my Doctoral degree. My mother joked about me being a permanent student because it seemed that I was always going to school. She lived to see me get two degrees. During my mid-fifties, I resumed my fourteen-year sidetracked quest and gained admission to the Virginia State University Doctoral degree program in Educational Administration and Supervision. Going back to school to fulfill my personal and professional goal was, for me, a more reasoned response to my midlife crisis than getting a tattoo.

It was all about timing. By this time in your life, you know life is short, and you live more urgently. Getting my last degree was something that I wanted to get done, and time was of the essence. I aspired to broaden my professional knowledge base and area of expertise with like-minded individuals who embraced a higher level of preparation, training, and study for advanced leadership opportunities. I was ready to integrate my life experiences as a career educator with advance study and research:

1. to enhance my intellectual understanding of human learning,
2. deepen my leadership capacities, and
3. accept the responsibility and expanded role of professional influence in the community by obtaining the highest degree in my profession.

The completion of my dissertation journey and conferred degree occurred a few years before I was sixty. As the clock ticked closer to me becoming a sexagenarian, careful planning and preparation allowed me to retire before hitting the big six zero. I am living my best life by regularly doing what I enjoy; including traveling, reading, staying active, having fun with fashion, appreciating my sensuality and femininity, finding humor and positive energy in life, socializing with friends and family, and being selfish enough to become the best version of myself. This same lesson I had learned so many years ago while learning to fry chicken is responsible for me maintaining my lifestyle.

Without a doubt, becoming sixty is an aging milestone, and aging is a phenomenon that cannot be denied; however, its definition has changed. As a woman in her sixties, I am living beyond the stereotypes of rocking chairs and floral housecoats, and I keep my makeup bag and daily moisturizers handy. There is an incredible amount of freedom and liberation of ideas, thoughts, actions, and appreciation during this phase. It is also a time that gives you space for reflection. By this time in our lives, we owe a measure of gratitude to someone who has made a difference in our lives. Who has lifted you onto their shoulders or stood by you in good and bad times? Think about your tribe, your champions, and supporters.

Along with your village, consider your adversaries and the naysayers. All have impacted and influenced your life in one way or another. What have you received from them? What have you learned on your journey? No matter how many twists and turns you may encounter as you travel the path of life, as each curve or experience unfolds, it brings greater meaning to your destiny. Each year between sixty and seventy is another opportunity to celebrate life to its fullest and accept responsibility for the choices, challenges, and changes that life's lessons teach each of us. Everyone is different and knowing what works for you and what you will do to remain relevant, passionate, and purposeful in life will define what you want to leave on the earth.

This will be *your* story.

ynthia Samuels Brown was born on December 24 in Fredericksburg, Virginia; the tenth of eleven children to Charles P. and Mary E. Samuels. Cynthia fulfilled her dream of becoming a teacher after her formal schooling and to this day; teaching remains one of her greatest passions. She is a retired school administrator with over 35 years of experience in the field of education. Cynthia worked as a classroom teacher, teacher mentor, assistant principal, and principal. Throughout her career, she had a reputation for high expectations, an uncompromising desire for excellence, and outstanding skills for communicating, organizing, and managing the social and educational development of others. Cynthia continues to be a highly effective scholar and visionary leader, a mentor for aspiring administrators and a role model for numerous other individuals. She is currently an Education Consultant. Her school teachers were among some of her early influencers and upon high school graduation, she attended Mary Washington University in Fredericksburg, Virginia for her undergraduate studies; earned her Masters in Education in Curriculum and Instruction at the University of Virginia in Charlottesville, Virginia and completed her doctoral studies at Virginia State University in Petersburg, Virginia.

Cynthia is an active and contributing member of the community in which she lives and has served on several boards in Arlington County while working diligently with other Board members to continue the mission and community impact of these organizations. Cynthia has an extensive background in volunteering and values the teamwork and collaboration board membership affords. She is a member of Our Lady Queen of Peace Catholic Church and serves as a Lector. Cynthia's life is further enriched by her membership in Delta Sigma Theta Sorority, Inc. She has been an active member since joining in April 1995. She is a member of the Northern Virginia Alumnae Chapter and has served in several leadership positions at the local and regional level. Cynthia is married to Bernard Brown and lives in Arlington, Virginia. She is the proud mother of her adult son Christopher and lives her best life by traveling, spending time with family and friends, cooking amazing recipes, re-reading some of her favorite books, going to the beach, and acknowledging her blessings.

Laura Dorsey, 66

The Music of My Life

Laura Dorsey

Recently, my daughter said to me, "The best thing that you ever did was to marry my daddy." If that is the case, let me tell you the story about the best thing that I ever did, by marrying Wallace Joe' Sugar' Dorsey. Since 'Sugar' loved music as much as I do, I am going to share our story by using music analogies.

I DID IT MY WAY

I do not like roller coaster rides, and I never have. You probably think that I mean the roller coaster that is a type of amusement park ride that employs a form of elevated railroad track designed with tight turns, steep slopes, and sometimes inversions. That is not exactly what I meant, but I do not like those either. I am talking about the roller coaster of life, which involves many emotional highs and lows or wonderful times alternating with difficult ones. By the time I turned twenty-one years old in 1975, my life had been a series of so many roller coasters that the average person would have been too dizzy to cope.

My twenty-first birthday was celebrated at Pete's Sportsman's Bar in Detroit with my sistah, Pat. Not really a partier, I was a waitress and barmaid, and Pat was the head barmaid. After escaping the domestic violence and being homeless, my Aunt Odessa, who was a social worker, helped me get on welfare so that I was able to get a place to stay for the girls and me. My son was living with his father. Knowing that welfare was not enough to support us, I found a job. I worked at night from 6:00 p.m. until 2:00 a.m. at the bar. That allowed me to be home with the girls during the day to make sure the eldest went to school. Around 5:00 p.m., after making sure they had dinner and were in pajamas, I took the girls downstairs. I lived on the third floor, in an apartment on the eastside of Detroit. My best friend, Liz, lived downstairs in the basement apartment, and she also managed the apartment building. I walked to the bus stop to catch the bus to work. I usually got a ride home because it was too late to catch the bus back.

July is usually the hottest month of the year in Detroit, with at least ten sunny days that bring nine hours of intense sunshine. The average high temperatures are in the scorching seventy-six to eighty-five-degree range. That type of heat made everyone irritable, especially my baby. By the time I got them settled, and downstairs to Liz, I had to run in the heat to catch the bus. If I missed it, I was going to be late for work while waiting for the next one. Liz was aware of my plight, and she had an idea. At the time, some renovations were going on in the building. She asked the person in charge if he would mind giving me a ride to work, letting him know that I only worked about thirty to forty-five minutes away. He agreed, indicating that he was done for the day anyway.

I met 'Sugar' Dorsey in July of 1975, and my life has not been the same since. He talked to me about my job, the girls, and life in general, as he drove me to work. Since he was done with work anyway, he decided to come to the bar and have a drink. He stayed for several hours. When he asked how I was going to get back home, I told him that I would get a ride and thanked him again for getting me to work on time. He left, but a few hours later, he had gone home and changed clothes and was back, listening to the band. He told me not to worry about getting home; he would wait and take me. I was so appreciative.

That was the last day that I ever took a bus to the bar or worried about getting home. He chauffeured me back and forth every day. 'Sugar' loved music and had previously had his own band, called 'Sugar' Dorsey's All-Stars. An accomplished guitar player, he usually sat in with the band when he was at the bar. There was only one problem with this friendship. The same year that I turned twenty-one years old, 'Sugar' Dorsey turned fifty-six.

A huge fan of fairy tales and Hallmark or Lifetime movies, I dreamed of a knight in shining armor coming to rescue me from the roller coaster ride of life. In my dreams, he was tall, dark, and handsome, but I do not remember how old he was in my dreams. I will tell you right now; be careful of what you ask God for because, as the scripture says, He will give you the desires of your heart. I wanted a man to love me and love my girls. I wanted a man that was kind, not violent, and financially secure enough so that I did not have to struggle. I wanted someone to take me off the roller coaster. 'Sugar' Dorsey checked off all of the boxes.

Consenting romantic relationships come in all shapes and sizes. However, when it comes to age differences between two people, reports show that most couples are born within three years of each other. This is likely because we meet our partners in places like school or entry-level jobs where everyone is around the same age. Although there can undoubtedly be obstacles for those relationships, they're not usually impacted by the number of candles on the birthday cake. The more significant impact happens with substantial age gaps between partners. Couples with an age gap between approximately five to fifteen years are estimated to make up eighty-five percent of the American population.

'Sugar' and I far exceeded that statistic. The challenges for age gap relationships are external, based on how others perceive them and internally as individuals deal with different life stages. The silver lining is that when couples work through age gap issues, studies find they can have greater marital satisfaction than similar-aged couples. According to research, when couples can identify their problems through the age difference and not a fractured love connection, the bond can be strengthened.

It's easy to say to forget about the haters, but the truth is that societal judgment makes its way into our private lives. Women can suffer from name-calling, such as gold-diggers. Men largely escape this type of shaming. 'Sugar' understood that society would influence my self-esteem and actively was my buffer when situations arose. For 'Sugar' and me, the biggest obstacle was my family. "How could you?" they asked. He was closer to my grandmother's age than mine - only four years younger. We had nothing in common. 'Sugar' was already working on his retirement, and I had never even started a career. He had money, and I did not. Moreover, he had children that were older than I was. It was never going to work, and I was crazy to think that it would.

A few years before I met 'Sugar', in 1969, Frank Sinatra popularized a song entitled 'My Way'. The song says:

I've loved, laughed, and cried, I've had my share of losing. And to think that I did it all and may I say not in a shy way, no, not me, I did it my way.

That became my theme song during this stage in my life. I did not care what anyone said or what anyone called me. I wanted to get off the roller coaster; my knight in shining armor came to my rescue, and I chose for my girls and me *to do it my way.*

WIND BENEATH MY WINGS

Not only was that July the last time that I caught the bus to work, but it was also the last time that I paid rent. It turns out that 'Sugar' had some connections with the owner of the building, and the rent was no longer a problem. I never again worried about enough food for the girls or diapers for the baby. There was nothing that I wanted that he did not provide for me. He took life to another level for me. I still worked at night, but my days were filled with fun. Remember Pat, from earlier in the story? Well, Pat is my sistah but not my biological sister. She is like the new Tyler Perry series, 'Sistahs' — you know — that friend that is closer than a sister. Yes, that is Pat. In the beginning, when 'Sugar' started taking me places, I had to admit the age difference still bothered me. I always took Pat with me. We laugh now, as we look back at that time. There was a day when 'Sugar' took us both shopping. We purchased similar outfits and thought we were the stuff. He took us to lunch in the dining room at the dog track. Neither of us had ever been. We watched from the box seats while we ate lunch. He gave us money to place a bet. We knew nothing about betting, but we set our bets based on the name of the horse, the name of the jockey, or the color that the horse had on its blanket. When one of our longshots won, we were over the moon. We made so much noise that people thought we had hit the trifecta. 'Sugar' just shook his head and laughed at us. It is a day that is etched in our memories.

I still worked at the bar. 'Sugar' asked me why I continued to work. I did not need to work; he reminded me. But I had been in a previous relationship when I did not work, and since I had no money, I had to suffer the abuse inflicted upon me. I promised myself that if I ever got out of that relationship, I would live by the words of my mother, who said, "God bless the child that has his own." We had moved by now, out of our apartment, first to Sugar's apartment and then to a flat. He took me to the furniture store, and we furnished the entire flat. I was truly living the fairytale, but I was determined to have my own spending money. The girls were in school, and we were comfortable. 'Sugar' had a plan. He reminded me that we were living in a middle-class neighborhood, so what would the girls say if someone asked them what their mother did for a living? I thought that being a barmaid was respectable. He did not. "If you still want to work, then find something that will make your daughters proud of you."

It has always been a saying that 'it is not what you know, but who you know'. That has always worked for 'Sugar'. At the bar, there were police officers who came in periodically, some regular guys from the plant in the neighborhood, and a few gentlemen that did not have nine to five jobs. He knew them all. I never questioned where my husband got his money. I do know that 'Sugar' has never had a real job. The band traveled across the United States before I met him. His family owned and operated an after-hours club. I do know that the liquor that was used came from questionable sources. Anyway, Craig was one of the police officers, plainclothes, so I am not sure what rank. We agreed that I would join the police department. He assured 'Sugar' that once I graduated from the academy, I would be placed inside at a desk. I liked the idea, so I signed up, passed the background and the physical, and prepared to start in two weeks. 'Sugar' was not as happy; he joked that it made little sense for someone who cried at every movie to be allowed to carry a gun. I was determined — unless he had a better plan. Of course, he did.

The Comprehensive Employment and Training Act (CETA) was a United States federal law to train workers and provide them with jobs in the public sector. There was a particular section of the program that paid for you to go to school, get a degree, and then get a job. They paid you to attend school, covered your childcare and necessary transportation expenses. There was a waiting list to get into this program, for most people, but not for 'Sugar' Dorsey. He made a telephone call. The next day, I was taking the assessment test to see whether I would attend college or a trade school. I have always been smart. My test scores indicated that I had an analytical ability with an emphasis on math.

The decision was that I would attend the Detroit Business Institute. 'Sugar' took the girls to school and then dropped me off at school daily. I was enjoying the experience. I asked to take day classes as well as night classes. I finished the two-year program in one and a half years. About the time that I was ready to graduate, I started putting in applications during my lunch hour. When I went to Detroit Bank & Trust, they asked me to stay and take an aptitude test. Of course, I could, after I called the school and told them I would be late. After the aptitude test, they asked if I could make myself available and stay for an interview. Okay, but remember, I am still a student. After the interview, they immediately offered me a position. I had two choices; I could either become a teller, or I could work in the subbasement in the securities area. I chose the securities area, but I reminded them that I still had two weeks left in this semester. They agreed to hold the job open for me. I started working at Detroit Bank & Trust in the Securities Trading/ Trust Operations Department on the Monday that I got out of school with an Associates in Business Administration. I still had another class, and I completed that at night. Of course, 'Sugar' was ecstatic. Actually, I was too.

Gerald Levert sings a song, entitled *Wind Beneath My Wings*. The lyrics say:

> *You were content to let me shine, that's your way*
> *You always walked a step behind*
> *See, I was the one with all the glory*
> *While you were the one with all the strength*
> *Only a face without a name*
> *I never once heard you complain. . .*
> *I could fly higher than an eagle*
> *'Cause you are the wind beneath my wings*

'Sugar' planted that desire in me to succeed. I started working with a mission to not only make my girls proud, but to make him proud also. I did not know anything about the stock market before going to work at the bank. I learned.

I worked my way from clerk to supervisor to manager. I took every class that the bank offered. I went to the University of North Carolina at Charlotte and earned a certificate in Trust Administration. Continuing to go to school at night, I entered Wayne County Community College and the University of Phoenix, earning another degree in Business Management and a Master of Art in Organizational Management. When I graduated from Wayne County, I purchased a class ring for 'Sugar'.

It was as much his degree as it was mine. He loved it, especially since he had never finished school, dropping out in the eighth grade to help take care of his family. I joke and say that he raised all of us. He took care of the girls, making sure they went to school, did homework, and ate. He did the grocery shopping and took care of the house. 'Sugar' woke up every morning and made sure that we had a hot meal before the girls went off to school, and I went off to work. My success was his success. When I left Comerica Bank (previously Detroit Bank & Trust), I was the Assistant Vice President of Trust Operations in San Jose, California. Always willing to sacrifice for my career, he allowed me to work in California. At the same time, he maintained our home in Detroit. He was indeed my hero, my knight in shining armor, *the wind beneath my wings.*

SIMPLE THINGS

"For so long, I didn't know I was searching in all the wrong places, spent more money than I could, if I worked harder than I should, always having friends to feel good, I'd be happier, losing my breath in the hustle, just stressing over nothing, forgetting the real joys that lie in the simple things."

Elisabeth Withers penned this song, and that is where I am in my life now. 'Sugar' passed away in March 2001, and there is not a day that I do not think about him. I am who I am because 'Sugar' Dorsey had a better vision for me than I had for myself. I know that he is proud of me, and the girls are too, which is what he wanted. While working on my Doctorate degree, I became a university professor, teaching English and Writing.

Now, in my Sexy Sixties, I have taken all of those skills to build a platform as the CEO of LLD Consulting, where I write for a variety of clients: Olympic athletes, attorneys, businesses — both for-profit and non-profit — and several national magazines. With all that I have achieved, I would trade it all for some time with 'Sugar' Dorsey to just enjoy *the simple things.* But knowing my knight in shining armor, he would not want my life to be any other way as I live my sexy sixties, enjoying the simple things with the wind beneath my wings and doing it my way!

*P*rofessor Laura Dorsey is the CEO of LLD Consulting, which specializes in taking your voice and the message that you want to convey and creating that written component that can be used in publications, speeches, and marketing and advertising. We also assist with sharing writing strategies for book manuscripts and magazine articles.

Professor Dorsey has a wide-ranging background in educational administration and corporate management. She has served as a University Academic Cabinet Member, SME General Education & English, and Area Chair: Academic Writing and General Studies in the College of Humanities for the University of Phoenix. Before her academic career, she had a very extensive career in financial services, retiring as Assistant Vice President of Trust Operations for Comerica Bank, responsible for merger/acquisitions, budgeting, and forecasting. Currently Laura serves as Communications Director for the Pan African Cultural Heritage Institute.

She is a member of the Central Florida Association of Black Journalists (CFABJ), an affiliate chapter of the National Association of Black Journalists (NABJ). She is the Associate Editor and contributing writer for both IBA Success Magazine and ONYX Magazine and a contributing writer for Program Success Magazine.

Laura is very involved in the community: board member and Vice President of the Southeast Region of Infinite Scholars Program; Board of Director's Treasurer for Clarita's House Outreach Ministry; Board of Directors Treasurer for Central Florida Diaper Bank; board member for YEP (Youth Empowerment Project). She is also a member of ABWA (American Businesswomen's Association). Professor Dorsey's career has led her to become a sought-after speaker on a variety of subjects.

Professor Laura Dorsey currently resides in the DMV, with her daughter and son-in-law, Tamika & Cecil Thomas. Her oldest daughter, Carolyn Diane Ross, two grandsons – Eric & Darrell, and great-granddaughter, Milah Tamika live on Long Island, New York.

Maeion Bryant, 62

MAEION'S STORY

Maeion Bryant

Most people have fond memories of their favorite decade. For me, it was during my childhood in Seattle, Washington. Growing up in the sixties was an exciting time for me. The culture of our community was rich with family values, and like many blessed children, I had fun — a lot of fun! However, when one grows up in a working-class family, struggle becomes a part of life. Outcomes of success, happiness, and other feelings of fulfillment depend on how one manages the struggles, the obstacles, and the challenges.

Therefore, I learned at an early age that the *grind* is important. Things would not be handed to me. If I wanted something, or if I wanted to be somewhere, I had to *grind* until I reached my goal. My sons have always said, "Ma, you're always on the *grind*." So, I believe that this underlying philosophy has framed my perspective on success.

My maternal inspiration came from my Aunt Mariah, who is my father's sister; it was her love and care that guided me through my challenging pre-teen years since my mother had passed away when I was two years old. So, it was Aunt Mariah who made sure we attended church and learned to cook. Being raised by such a brave and classy woman has been beneficial because, through her actions, the seeds of empowerment were sown into my soul. Helping other women develop personal confidence and strength through self-awareness and beauty would become my lifetime passion and purpose.

I became interested in beauty and hair care at an early age. I was only nine years old when I began earning money while styling hair for neighbors in the community, making me an entrepreneur long before I understood the true meaning of the word. In middle school, I convinced my father to pay my admittance fee for a local charm school — a good move for me at a critical time in my life. I was eager and ready to learn valuable lessons about life while gaining knowledge about personal etiquette. The classes taught best practices in self-care, posture, walking, and communication. Learning these subjects helped me to better understand what it truly meant to be a woman in our society.

When I started high school, we were well into the seventies; music was transitioning, color television increased in popularity, big beautiful afros took center stage, and a proud Black presence emerged across our nation. Although struggles continued to exist for Black people, we were finally telling ourselves that we were beautiful and strong, showing love to each other and our community. Like so many other James Brown fans, I said it loud, "I'm Black and I'm proud!" Unfortunately, white society was not so eager to support our newfound self-awareness, continuing to dismiss our accomplishments, our beauty, and our worth. Nevertheless, I did not need their approval. I had already found and accepted my inner beauty, so I wanted to project it outwardly, showing other Black women that we had a place in the beauty world.

After receiving etiquette lessons, I enrolled in a fashion program through the Patricia Stevens Institute. In addition to providing excellent modeling lessons, the instructor taught me useful makeup skills that would eventually become the cornerstone of my career as a makeup artist.

Initially, my passion was not applying makeup. It was modeling. Walking down that runway was my dream, but unfortunately, my dream did not come easily because reality presented many obstacles, including family, the need to work, and the challenges of living on my own. So instead, I decided to continue my secondary education at Seattle Central Community College, concentrating on business administration, art, and other electives that fit into my career plans. Still, it was difficult for me to keep up with my demanding schedule, but I persisted, and through that persistence, I crossed paths with an exceptional individual, Frankie Williams, who owned a modeling studio in Seattle. It did not take long for us to become friends, and over time, our trusting friendship evolved, with Frankie transitioning to the roles of both mentor and agent.

While Frankie hustled, I remained on the *grind*, with my hard work eventually paying off. I began modeling and was exposed to the continuous beat that existed in the fashion industry — the movement, the change, the vibrancy, the stories, and the never dormant state of trends. Fashion became my *grind*, and I modeled full-time for prominent retailers in the Seattle area, such as Nordstrom, Frederick & Nelson, I. Magnin, The Bon Marché, and others. But I desired to expand on my experiences, so I pursued other opportunities using my industry knowledge. At one point, I took on the role of Head Fashion Coordinator for a local bridal show and a premier "Back to School" fashion show. These events offered me both experience *and* exposure. The shows were quite successful, and they provided the funds I needed to finance my next endeavor because, although I loved Seattle, I still craved more of the world.

I used my savings from the shows to travel to Europe with two other models from the modeling agency, Linda Johnson and Julie Bowen. We were excited about our international venture, which took us to London and Paris. The experience was invaluable, providing insight and rapid growth in the fashion industry. High-end shoots, bright lights, big stages, runway shows, and world-class designers were daily aspects of my life. But even in this glorious, fast-paced European world, I encountered difficulties. See, in the United States, the Black spirit had been lifted, laws had been enacted, and we had almost overcome, yet there was still a lack of social acceptance and professional confidence among people of color, particularly within white-dominated industries, including fashion. By fashion, I mean all aspects: beauty, makeup, designers, models, stylists, magazine, print, and photographers. Europe was no exception to this socially misguided and misinformed state of mind. So, let's just say, it was challenging for Black models to get work in the seventies — nationally and globally.

After spending a few months abroad, I returned to Seattle, where I met and married Lou Bryant. We moved to southern California, where I connected with a new modeling agency. Through this agency, I continued my runway and print work for Nordstrom, Saks Fifth Avenue, and Macy's. It was during this period that I had an epiphany: *The same old faces were being recycled over and over throughout the industry.* Many were older, white models who had been around for years, and there were very few black or young faces.

So, I took steps to correct this imbalance. I opened a modeling studio and trained models on how to walk the runway, pose for shoots, professionally style hair, and professionally apply makeup. Word eventually got around that I was doing something new and fresh; retail stores, such as Nordstrom, began to refer models to my studio so that I could adequately prepare them for their desired style. While running the studio, I also worked as a stylist on local commercials and print jobs for *San Diego Magazine*. I soon began to enjoy the hustle behind the camera and considered yet another career adjustment; however, life once again, interrupted my plans. My husband and I moved from one coast to the other, relocating from San Diego to Maryland in 1985, when Lou received a new job promotion, and I was pregnant with our first son.

The birth of our eldest son, Louis, Jr., brought a new perspective of joy to our lives. Becoming a mom meant a new type of *grind*, managing the role of mother and career woman. It was imperative that I not

give up on my career. I wanted both. So, as we watched Lou, Jr. grow into an energetic toddler, I continued doing what I knew best — networking.

In 1986, I enrolled in the *Von Lee School of Aesthetics*, eventually receiving certification as a professional makeup artist. I also continued to model, which led to my participation in the promotional fashion show for the grand opening of the Tyson's Corner Mall in Northern Virginia. Locally, this was a major event. Professionally, it was a career-changing opportunity, but the experience itself was a little "bumpy" because the other models did not want to share the runway with me. I was an outsider, and every bump and nudge that I received on the catwalk that night was a clear message of disapproval. There was an established clique that seemed to be impenetrable. It was apparent that I would not be accepted in their circle, but their rejection did not stop my *grind*. I simply altered my career strategy once again.

I reached out to numerous ad agencies and photographers in the marketplace. Luckily, the response was warm, and people supported my services. Soon, my client list grew, and I received calls from photographers and production companies all over the Mid-Atlantic region. From 1988 to 1995, I worked in the Cosmetics Department for Neiman Marcus, learning the basics of running a makeup counter. I also freelanced my services outside of the store.

In 1990, our youngest son, Keenon, was born, and we were once again elated about expanding our family size. The culmination of all of my experiences — blended with the mistakes and lessons I had learned along the way — awoke a desire to approach work from a different angle. In 1999, I took a leap of faith and became a full-time entrepreneur, focusing on makeup and cosmetic services. The *grind*, combined with my networking abilities, allowed me to fully transition to an entrepreneurial existence by creating a new business entity: *Maeion Bryant Cosmetics.*

As a business owner in the beauty industry, I have been given incredible opportunities to connect with key industry players. I contracted as a brand manager for Queen Latifah's makeup line through *Cover Girl Cosmetics* during the Sugar Water Festival from 2006 to 2008. Cover Girl also contracted me to coordinate the makeup for the 2008 Miss USA Pageant. My chair has seated brides, musicians, dancers, career professionals, and numerous celebrities, including Aretha Franklin, James Earl Jones, Chris Tucker, Danny Glover, Ava DuVernay, Gloria Steinem, and Misty Copland. Currently, I work with a variety of production companies, media outlets, and photographers such as PBS News Hour, BET News NY, and CNN. Additionally, I have worked on multiple short films when I created zombies and aging characters using special effects makeup.

For many years, I worked in the traditional sense of business, primarily operating through set appointments and studio visits. I also earned money by remotely providing my services, often packing up most of my studio essentials to provide makeup services on production sets, at wedding venues, at community centers, and private locations. The physical address of my makeup studio frequently changed, as the prices of rent continued to rise year after year. As a result, some clients jokingly commented that it would be better if I could just bring my services to their front door. Another seed was planted. In 2016, Lou and I purchased a used assisted mobility van, which we customized based on my specifications. The result of this grand effort was a makeup studio — on wheels! My customers loved it! This innovative studio offered my customers convenience, comfort, and style. With my new wheels, I could meet my customers in almost any location at any time, offering personalized services and attention.

Under the business label *Maeion Beauty & Company, LLC,* I manage a team of professional makeup artists. This team is available for individual sessions or large groups and collectively offered a wide range of services, including wedding preparations, individual makeup lessons, wardrobe styling, brow grooming, and corporate image branding. We also offer custom blending services when we personalize the client's makeup using my mineral foundations.

As a makeup artist and an active participant in the skincare world, I often promoted standard messaging about skincare. One should always have a personalized skincare regime to promote healthy, radiant skin. The use of toxic chemicals will eventually wear down the skin, instead of providing the essential nutrients and vitality that the skin truly needs. To help clients with their skincare concerns, I promoted my own organic skincare line. Products such as *CC Serum* with Vitamin C, and *Cucumber Herbal Eye Gel* with hyaluronic acid, shea, and botanical extracts are two products that enhanced the skin through natural ingredients. I enjoy educating my clients on how to take care of themselves from head to toe, suggesting regular facials, massages, hair care, nail care, and thirty minutes of "me" time daily, and emphasizing that this routine be a priority.

Helping women develop personal confidence and strength through self-awareness and beauty is how I chose to "pay it forward". It is also how I choose to give thanks for the good deeds and opportunities that I have received from others. My donations of time have been utilized in a variety of ways. I assisted women who were Hurricane Katrina victims, applying their makeup, and helping build their self-confidence as they prepared to re-enter the job market. I conducted workshops for women in shelters. I participated in job training programs, teaching women the proper way to wear makeup and dress for job interviews. I donated numerous hours working with young ladies in programs; such as the United Way of Maryland and the Department of Social Services, teaching etiquette, beauty training, and confidence-building techniques. I also encourage women to always be conscious of how they look and how they feel because makeup is a powerful tool that can be beneficial when used correctly. I do not promote makeup as a necessity, but more as an accessory — a way to enhance confidence and celebrate beauty on the inside and the outside — as it will not correct health issues, and in most cases, it will not hide them.

So, my advice regarding makeup is simple: Wear what makes you comfortable, whether you enjoy the full glam approach or prefer a subtle natural touch. Always wash and remove your makeup. Stop eating processed foods. Eat food that has good nutritional value, limiting starches, preservatives, and sugar. Get seven hours of sleep. Keep track of your blood pressure. And, take care of "you", head to toe, not just your face.

Finally, I have referred to my *grind* over and over. I have done so because it has been my single source of motivation along my journey. My *grind* fuels my energy level, but I manage this by continually reminding myself that I can only control "me" and that includes *both my actions* and my *reactions* to the behaviors of others. My motto is: *Don't get upset until you know the outcome. Otherwise, you are wasting energy.* And, if you are wasting energy, you are wasting time.

Over the years, I have collected tidbits of wisdom that I have used throughout my life. Some of those tidbits or personal lessons include the following:

- Follow your steps with a clear vision.
- Don't let naysayers keep you from your passion.
- Surround yourself with positive people in your life and those who support your interests.
- Keep grinding through the struggle.
- Maintain a positive outlook on life because there will always be obstacles.
- Ignore distractions because they will come.
- Stay focused on your inner conscience for direction.
- Know that you will succeed.

As we begin this new decade, I am embracing my *sexy sixties* with enthusiasm and optimism. I am excited about what is ahead, and I look forward to witnessing some of the wondrous achievements that are yet to come for women in all industries, not just the beauty and fashion industries. I anticipate more growth, more grinding, and a new era filled with never-ending passion from all women.

It's an exciting time to be sixty!

Maeion Bryant grew up in Seattle, Washington in the sixties. Her love for enhancing a person's beauty today came at the early age of nine years old. She began by styling neighbors hair which gave her joy and excitement, and her compensation was fresh baked cookies! As she grew into a young lady, she learned so much about her new field and met wonderful people along the way, who helped develop her fashion and beauty career she loves so much today.

Maeion met her husband, Lou Bryant, in her early twenties in Seattle, Washington. They later relocated to San Diego, CA. During her three years of living in San Diego she continued modeling and making contacts. She opened a successful modeling program and began training professional models. Her husband received a promotion on his job which moved them to Columbia, MD in the early eighties. They raised two amazing sons, Louis the 3rd and Keenon along with their niece, Casisunay.

Maeion continued her education in the beauty industry and received her certification at Von Lee International School of Aesthetics. She also received training in theater makeup at Community College of Baltimore County (CCBC). By working at Neiman Marcus and other major department stores she gained valuable makeup skills and learned important lessons on how to become a successful entrepreneur. She now owns and operates Maeion Beauty & Company, a fully equipped makeup studio on wheels which is used to serve clients on demand with their beauty & styling needs. Maeion consistently works with many professional media outlets in the Washington, D.C. and surrounding area. She provides makeup & hair styling services for professional clients for television commercials, special events, photo shoots with photographers, and serve national news stations.

Maeion takes pride in giving countless hours of service to organizations like United Way of Maryland and the Department of Social Services. She has donated business hours to Roberta's House of Baltimore, Job Core, and Good Shepherd School for Girls. Maeion saw the need for young ladies ages 10 - 13 to have positive self esteem so she developed an 8 week Summer Sewing and Fashion program for them.

Maeion also believes in taking care of her temple! With meditation, eating healthy, and routine check- ups, she will maintain a healthy lifestyle in her sixties and beyond, along with having a sexy body!

Sylvia Garrett, 68

REFINED BY AGE

Sylvia Garrett

> *"Now is the best time to assess whether the lenses*
> *in our aging attitude glasses need an adjustment."*
> *-Kathy Sporre*

The above quote made me stop and think, *"Wow... this is so profound!"* What thoughts do I have on the aging process and society's perception of growing old? Having worked with seniors during my career, what, now, was my perception – and what wisdom had I learned – if any? Reflecting, I recalled a married couple, the wife at ninety-nine, and her wheelchair-bound husband at one hundred and two, both made such an impression on me. They live with their daughter, who worked and was the caregiver of her adult disabled daughter. The daughter had a lot on her plate, so she needs some assistance for her elderly parents now.

The wife was beautiful, with long flowing gray hair against her mocha skin. Raised in the mid-west, she had been a seamstress, was civic-minded and socially active, and had many stories to share with me. I loved hearing the stories, staying during my visits much longer than expected. What I remember most was the wife's sense of purpose and her desire to teach girls how to sew, which she felt was becoming a lost art. Even at almost one hundred years of age, her internal motivation was to remain active and to continue to make a difference throughout her life's journey. I liked this about her.

SELF-AWARENESS

It's been said that there are advantages and disadvantages at any age. That may be true. The joy of being in your sixties is the ability to sit back and laugh at how self-conscious many of us once were. Now we smile in our confidence, beauty (inside and out), and God's grace. Isn't it great that we don't have to subscribe to negative aging stereotypes about how we should dress and what our hairstyles should look like? Who says "sexy" has an expiration date? I contend that it doesn't. Feeling good and looking beautiful as we age is certainly possible.

Personally, an awareness of my purpose in life was realized on August 28, 1963, while sitting in the kitchen watching the black and white portable television with my Mom. On that day, we were watching the March on Washington, led by Dr. Martin Luther King, Jr. and others. The event title was "March on Washington for Jobs and Freedom" when Dr. King gave his iconic "I Have a Dream" speech at the Lincoln Memorial. It has been estimated that 250,000 people participated. At age eleven, I was totally mesmerized by what I saw on the television that day. I can remember wanting so much to be present at the march, knowing that, due to proximity, I had no way to get there. My parents weren't going to take me, especially since Mom –being of a protective nature – feared possible violence could erupt. Nevertheless, I decided that even if I couldn't be there physically, I could be there in spirit.

On this epic summer day, I knew my purpose in life would be to help others.

By having self-awareness, engaging in self-care, reflecting on lessons learned, and embracing positive connections, you can have a positive aging experience. As demonstrated by the older woman I spoke of previously, we cannot subscribe to the limits and stereotypes society wants to attach to a certain age. Do you know who you are? Do you recognize your uniqueness? You are the author of your life, so be yourself; everyone else is already taken. At no time should you forget who you are and the unique qualities you possess.

> *"I can't be you. You can't be me…"*
> *-John Green*

It's just as important not to let others, who may be critical or judgmental, define you. Never let others have the power to define your happiness or sense of worth. My responsibility is to remind myself of who I am. That's why I love the Coco Chanel quote, "Beauty begins the moment you decide to be yourself."

Embracing my sexy sixties is about my self-awareness, knowing who I am, having a positive attitude on life with a defined purpose. And, although I am still a work in progress, this positive outlook has helped in accomplishing my dreams and goals.

Sexy Sixties Nuggets:
1. Pray daily and be grateful and joyful.
2. Be comfortable in your own skin.
3. Meditate on positive mental visualizations of your dreams and goals (it's never too late).
4. Speak positive affirmations.

SELF-CARE

Like many women, I married and raised a family in pursuit of a happy, healthy, and stable family life — my new *why*— becoming a master juggler of my family life and career and having little time for myself.

However, if you are like me, embrace your sixties and make time for the things you have always wanted to do. Learn a foreign language, read more, take that class, travel to broaden your horizons and perspectives. As a member of the personal development community, I enjoy learning, as it helps me with building my business. I watch many videos on YouTube and enjoy watching the sunrise during my travels. Currently, I'm studying to take the Project Management Professional (PMP) Certification exam. Why? Because I want to! And, because I like being able to share what I have learned with others.

You will also want to eat healthy and drink plenty of water; drinking thirty-two ounces, at room temperature first thing in the morning, helps to flush your body of toxins. Get on a good sleep routine, and don't forget to exercise, ladies!

Skincare is very important to your personal self-care regimen. Always moisturize dry skin and use sunscreen when outside. I use a THC-free, hemp-derived CBD anti-aging moisturizer from my *Oxzgen* product line.

Lastly, remember to pamper yourself by doing something special to celebrate your fabulous self. I like this quote by Bishop T.D. Jakes, *"If you celebrate yourself, others will come to your party."*

Sexy Sixties Nuggets:
1. Become your own self-advocate.
2. Now is the time to focus on your wants and needs.

LIFE LESSONS LEARNED

We have all had our share of successes and failures. No one can reach their sixties without experiencing both! So, now is the time to start building on your life experiences — the lessons learned and the wisdom gained from your life's journey. For many of us, it has not been, as some say, a bed full of roses; but, isn't life about how we have overcome the trials and tribulations we have encountered? Hopefully, the lessons learned have made us better — not bitter, because it's how we respond to our experiences that can either break us down or make us stronger.

> *"There are no mistakes*
> *in life, only lessons."*
> *-Robin S. Sharma*

Life has knocked me down a few times, but I always got back up. I have experienced many lessons, such as in my career, friendships, marriage, parenthood, singlehood, business relationships, money, religion, spirituality, and familiar conflicts — just so many. However, I will share one with you; at age fifty, my marriage of twenty-one years had crumbled. As in most marriages, there were great times, our children, memorable vacations, and joyful holidays. Both my husband and I loved *and* cherished our two wonderful sons, Robert and Spencer. One of our core values was to always be there for them, so we were actively involved in their schools, sports, and scouting programs.

Then, there were unpleasant times, with unresolved issues of communication being one. As a couple, we had become, as they say, 'like ships that pass in the night.' His busy traveling schedule offered a higher family income, but less time at home. My job was equally demanding, many times requiring long, uncompensated hours. Somehow, we always made time for our kids' activities. Rarely was there a time my kids experienced a parent not present for an activity; however, with the many demands on us, our marriage was in trouble, and I prayed for change — more God-centered time, more couple time, and much better communication. God answered my prayer, but not in the way I had envisioned. Still, a tremendous burden had been lifted from my shoulders.

The end of a marriage is painful, and there is a true feeling of loss. It wasn't like love was not there, but that we were just unable to find our way, together. This experience truly helped shape me into embracing my sixties.

My decision to start a part-time direct sales business was the second biggest impact on my life. At the time, I was also working a part-time job. However, what I do, now, in my business has nothing to do with what I learned in school, but through the business, I've learned so much; it has given me fresh perspectives, increased my sense of focus and direction, and provided me with clarity on my purpose in life. I have also learned that I deserve more in life for myself and my children, along with how I love to experience the joy of helping others reach their fullest potential in life, which helps me to wake up every morning with a positive outlook.

After all of this, the greatest lesson I've learned is the importance of FORGIVENESS – and this has supported me in embracing my sixties.

Sexy Sixties Nuggets:
1. Have compassion for unconditional forgiveness, including forgiving ourselves.
2. Keep a positive attitude and accepting what I cannot change.

HEROES AND SHEROES

My parents were my first role models and true blessings in both my happy times and the most difficult times. Due to my marital separation, unknowingly, God had blessed me by letting me spend precious time with my Mom – for, just in a few months, my heart was broken. Just seven months and nine days after her seventy-fourth birthday, my mother passed away.

Her last words to me were, "Will you be okay by yourself?" I told her, "Yes, I will be fine." I knew that I had God by my side and that she would always be there for me. At the time, however, I didn't really know what she meant.

Let me tell you about my Mom . . . she enjoyed being a Mom. Coming from a broken home, she loved being married and having a family; each of her four children were special to her. I, being the only girl, was told just how much she had wanted me — a girl. She worked in a government job, yet housekeeping was very important, too. Her home was her castle. Although Mom married and changed her mind about pursuing a college education, she believed in higher education and women becoming economically self-sufficient. Both she and my Dad were happy with my decision to attend college, for neither of them had done so, even though my Dad, a 'numbers' man, had attended business school while working his government job. Still, he had gradually worked his way up from being a clerk to clerk-typist and then eventually a budget analyst, while in his successful career in a Defense Department federal agency.

Dad was also an athlete and highly competitive. As an avid tennis player, I loved Dad's competitiveness. He was able to play tennis year-round, well into his eighties. It was only after a problem with his toe – and being a Type 2 diabetic – that he had to become an inactive "super senior." I know he missed playing tennis with his friends. Several years ago, he went to his heavenly home, and like Mom, he will always remain in my heart.

Outside of family, my first hero was American tennis player, Arthur Robert Ashe, Jr. He was a former number one American professional tennis player and the first African American man to be ranked number one in the world.

I was sixteen years old when my Dad took me to 16th and Kennedy Street to a tennis tournament. I remember seeing Arthur Ashe, Jr. up close and in person. I was so elated. I later learned that he was a young black man, born in the south, who had become a professional tennis player, which helped break down racial barriers in the sport of tennis; he was an activist. As a young kid, I can recall the buzz, but did not fully understand it at that moment. My Dad was playing against Ashe, then a college student. No, Dad did not win his match, but he was proud to have that opportunity to play against this rising, young black tennis star.

My Dad was an active member of the American Tennis Association (ATA). It's the oldest African American sports organization in the United States. The organization was borne out of racism over a century ago when the U.S. Lawn Tennis Association barred African American players. Ashe came through the ranks of the ATA, as other players that followed.

Some of my *sheroes* include former First Lady Michelle Obama; she is such an inspiration, intelligent, classy, and beautiful. I must also mention Oprah Winfrey; I love Oprah's saying, "The way I see it . . . every year can be a brand-new journey." That is such a great thought.

I am so inspired by Ernestine Shepherd, who was known at one point in the Guinness World Record Book for being the oldest competitive female bodybuilder in the world. At eighty-three years old, she is a true inspiration. I was able to participate in one of her exercise classes at my workplace in Baltimore, probably around twelve years ago. I enjoyed coming to her weekly class with soft jazz music playing. Certainly, a respite from a hectic workday, even if only for an hour.

She is an inspirational woman of color, who embraced her age in her fifties to become more and to reach her fullest potential.

There have been so many more people who have had an impact throughout my life that I can't mention them all, but I am so grateful our paths crossed.

Sexy Sixties Nuggets:
1. Have the right positive connections.
2. Be mentored and mentor others.
3. Identify your sheroes and heroes.
4. When the right people enter your life, positive things will begin to happen.

There are many things I still desire to do *and* to accomplish for my community, my family, and myself. I'll push forward and continue to move with God's grace. Now, at sixty-seven years young, I feel young in spirit with a sense of gratitude — knowing God's grace shines upon me. And, my perception on aging is well-stated by blogger, Kathy Spoore:[1]

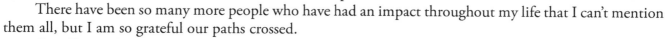

"I will be refined by age, not defined by it."

Life will *always* be complicated. Nevertheless, remain positive, be joyful, and happy as you age fabulously and gracefully. Be the person you know you are; confident, beautiful, and sexy. By walking in the God-given purpose we were each created for, it will bring about ultimate joy and fulfillment in life. So, I say to you . . . know yourself and walk in your purpose.

Let's embrace our sexy sixties!

---

[1] Kathy Sporre @ www.refinedbyage.com

Sylvia Garrett is an Entrepreneur in direct sales that offers home and business services, as well as, health and wellness products, providing positive results. Her passion for helping other spans over 40 years. She worked in human service programs during her successful career as a human service professional and retired as a Program Administrator. Today, she devotes much of her time to her business. Sylvia calls her business her Ministry as she walks in her God given purpose of helping others. She especially enjoys her senior customers. Sylvia loves the positive experience of knowing she has helped others feel better and look better.

Sylvia holds a Bachelor of Science degree in Sociology, with a concentration in Social Welfare, from Hampton University (1975). She completed graduate course work at Howard University School of Social Work. She received a Masters of Arts degree in 1996 in Management/ Public Administration. Currently she studies for Project Management Professional Certification.

Sylvia is the mother of two sons, a Health Advocate, and is known for her volunteerism. She is a member of Sisters 4 Sisters Network, Inc.

Sylvia Headen Douglin, 67

ARRIVAL AND UNDERSTANDING

Sylvia Headen Douglin

When I was a child in the fifties and sixties, I wondered what it would be like to be a grown-up lady. The images on TV and movies showed young women in beautiful clothes, hair coifed, and vacuuming in high heels while wearing their pearls. My mother and her friends all fit that mold as well – elegant, proper, beautifully dressed (but no heels and pearls while cleaning – they were, after all, black women and had a more practical approach to housework). This is what I knew and aspired to. This is how I wanted to present myself.

I wanted to be like THEM.

We wore the white gloves and hats to church at Easter, and pretty dresses for fancy occasions while we were little girls, then we began to grow up. Not only did WE change into adolescents, but the world had moved, quite prominently, into the sixties, and the symbols morphed. The fur stoles, white gloves, petticoats, and hats were gone; replaced by miniskirts, go-go boots, afros, and maxi coats — a complete shift. Despite those changes, my idea of what a grown-up woman should be remained well-defined by watching my mother — elegant, proper, and beautifully dressed. Those things did not change — what did change was HOW they were pictured. Carnaby Street became fashion's north star, which was how young women (and men) wanted to look, not like the 'new look' of the post-war fifties. The British invasion influenced more than music; it influenced style as well.

Throughout my young and middle years, I used the lessons learned about how to physically present myself as a modern woman. There were LOTS of examples of fashionable women in my age group. Fashion, in general, was expanding to include more women. Diane von Furstenberg's wrap dress made just about every woman look GREAT – even curvy black women. Suddenly, there were black women in the fashion world that we could emulate. Pat Cleveland, Beverly Johnson, and Mounia (muse for Yves St. Laurent, Karl Lagerfeld, and Emanuel Ungaro) were on the runways and magazine covers. Essence magazine became a vehicle for ideas and fashion. We could see ourselves!

The other fundamental lessons came from my mother and her circle of friends who represented elegance and sophistication to me. Mom taught me both how to BE and LOOK confident, and those ladies showed me how to carry it off! My sister and I were the tallest girls in our neighborhood. I was five feet seven inches tall in the sixth grade with two inches still to grow; all of the other girls were at least three inches shorter. I was skinny with glasses before Twiggy made skinny popular, long before glasses were a fashion accessory, and before contacts were comfortable. My mother insisted that we 'stand up straight' to embrace our full height. She told us that we were the Headen Girls, and as a result, we learned to move in the world with our heads held high, even though it was a few years before we were no longer looking *over* the heads of the rest of the neighborhood.

She encouraged my LOVE of fashion - not by buying every new trend (that didn't happen back in the day), but by understanding my need for the white go-go boots and not *dis*couraging their purchase. During these years, I also learned how style could be an individual expression, not wholly dictated by others. I learned to stand out and emulate the Motown stars; the beautiful dresses and hair of the Supremes and Martha Reeves and the Vandellas. I also began to understand the signature style of the Temptations, Miracles, and The Four Tops, who showed a generation of black youth how to step out. Then we turned all of that on its head and tie-dyed our way into our early twenties. All of these examples came, blended, and then went throughout the decades. I navigated the twenty-first century with all of these examples. The questions came after the turn of this new millennium. How does one move forward and STAY in the game of modern life AFTER you cross that mid-century threshold? All of the previous iterations of style, life, sexiness, and contribution came with the same 'faces' —those of young women.

What had *not* been shown in all of those prior models and scripts were the older women. The women who had raised their children, buried loved ones, and lived some life, were relegated to the sidelines. They were, of course, at church, involved in community events, part of raising all of the neighborhood children, and held in high regard. Still, they were considered helpers, supporters, and most importantly, *believed to have already lived their lives. Their active life was behind them.* Society didn't expect or encourage women to be vibrant after motherhood — and definitely not after becoming a grandmother. In fact, life beyond motherhood was actively discouraged. As a result, there were virtually no examples of older women still embracing a vibrant or adventurous life beyond their youth. There were even fewer, if any, examples of older women of high standing and accomplishment who were still considered sexy. To this day, being sexy as an

older woman is deemed to be tawdry, uncouth, or predatory, as sexiness is only relegated to the erotic. But we now recognize that sexiness also relates to emotional stimulation, appeal, and excitement. Women can retain these qualities throughout their life – well into and beyond sixty. Having a zest for life is timeless and profoundly sexy.

My whole life has had image at its center. I grew up in fashion. I spent years modeling, designing clothing, and teaching women how to present themselves effectively. Fashion has always been directed toward that standard I grew up with; that INCLUDED the young and EXCLUDED those who were not. Anyone over the age of forty was considered a 'has-been', past her prime, and subjected to a backseat for the remainder of her life. Those outdated concepts have now reinvented to allow the 'woman of a certain age' to participate in the world more expansively. She no longer has to be ONLY Mommy or ONLY Granny. She can be those things and whoever else she wants to be and can express that in whatever way she chooses.

Now, I have reached the stage when I have raised my children and buried some loved ones. I am officially an 'old lady' (card-carrying AARP member); however, the paradigm of the old lady has moved away from 'sideline dweller' to taking the reins for a second (or third) act. We live in a way that cannot be accomplished by the young – their energy, while powerful, is different. Young people's energy is full of new experiences and wonder. Our energy is full of wisdom, a world view, and a life lived. That energy is now being expressed in the world with examples of women who hold and own the stage of life that they are on. In their sixties, Angela Bassett, Sharon Stone, Grace Jones, Sheryl Lee Ralph, Cyndi Lauper are still stopping shows. Debbie Allen has gone from dancer to producer —choosing another branch of the well-worn and successful path we are used to seeing her on.

Cher and Patti LaBelle continue to sell out venues in their seventies. Tina Turner and Jane Fonda redefined what's possible for women in their eighties. Cicely Tyson and Iris Apfel continue to hone their respective crafts at well over ninety years on the earth. Tyson won a Tony Award at eighty-nine and was an Emmy Nominee at ninety-four. Apfel started a successful accessory line in her mid-nineties, and now, has her own Barbie Doll! These are some of the myriad examples we now have of women who not only EMBRACED their sixth, seventh, eighth, or ninth decade of life, but also squeezed every bit of excitement from it. BOLD Ladies, all!

Now that I, too, am a *BOLD lady*, I'm exploring the world anew with a perspective not available to the young.

I've been around the block – more than once. I've also watched others circle this block called life and learned, or adapted, from their spin. I am among the women who are here to change that old paradigm of the sweet old lady who needs help crossing the street. WE are the BOLD ladies who are building, growing new wings, and contributing to life in ways that are astute and based on more than theory. The wisdom gained in those trips around the block, informs HOW I move into and through the future. This is the new part of my life to be embraced – turning those familiar corners and finding 'new construction' built since the last time around, that have obliterated those old guideposts that everyone thought would always be there. It makes living scary, exhilarating, appealing, attractive, arousing, and SEXY. To BE in this sexy new world, I think you must jump in with both feet and use the experience gained through life to interpret and apply what's new to what's already known. To be part of the world going forward, you have to embrace it and hang on tight.

HOW I EMBRACE MY SEXY SIXTIES

A sexy woman, at any age, is not only about romance and skinny thighs. A *sexy* woman is a woman who is taking control of her life, her body, her contributions to the world. Women who KNOW they are sexy, move through the world with confidence and excitement. Think of Oprah Winfrey (age sixty-six), Vera Wang (age seventy), and Helen Mirren (age seventy-four) who are still strutting their stuff, blazing new trails, taking on more and different challenges and continuing to make their marks in their chosen industries across the globe.

I feel CONFIDENT in my sixties. For me, that confidence comes from taking care of myself, FOR MYSELF – not to please or take direction from others -- because I WANT TO and because **I** matter to ME – the BOLD lady. As I enjoy the sixties and look toward the future decades, I feel EXCITED because there are so many possibilities and new paths around that familiar old block I've been around, that will take me into new places. I express myself to the world through clothing — I always have. I find it is as vital now, as it was when I was a young woman — just that now, it's a different expression. That expression is now one of the continued connections to times and life around me. That expression is one of vitality, tempered, and honed by the years. That expression is that of the BOLD Lady.

You have fifteen seconds from first sight until adults categorize you and put you in a mental 'box' (that's not because they are being judgmental; it's just the way the adult brain works). That understanding makes me think about how I am presenting, whenever I'm out and about. One of my favorite statements is, "There's no such thing as *I'm only going*." There absolutely is no such thing to me! When I make that quick run to CVS or to go to get some gas, this standard is not overlooked. Why does it matter; why should I care? Because you never know who you'll encounter on that 'quick run' — the ex, the colleague, the potential client, your arch enemy, or maybe someone 'fascinating'. You just never know. I'm not saying that every trip to the dollar store is an occasion for full makeup and fancy clothing. I am saying that, no matter what the 'trip', you should look like you care about yourself, your place in the world, and how you are seen.

For me, it means that my clothing is real clothing (not pajamas), sweats, and t-shirt are neat and reflect today's world, not a pink tracksuit from the eighties that says, 'I'm stuck in the past.' Because of quick sorting that adults do, I know I WILL be placed into a box, but I can influence the label that gets put on it. I prefer my appearance to say that I am part of the modern world — that I'm not that doddering old lady that needs help. It says that she's part of today, she knows what she's doing, and she is not to be marginalized or put in the corner'. Looking good makes you feel good; you walk taller and stand straighter. Looking your best or, at least put together for those CVS runs, gives you that little extra confidence needed when facing the unfamiliar, trying something new, or just getting out there and being in the game. You can know that you have controlled all you can, now take a deep breath and keep going. You just never know who you will meet or influence, and it DOES matter.

I wear what I wear because I choose to represent myself. I choose STYLE over FASHION. Fashion is someone else's idea of what we should look like 'this season' – whether it looks good on you, someone else or not. Style is showcasing who YOU are and dressing in a manner that expresses you NOW. We have all seen women who chase fashion trends. Every season, they try to keep up with what's on the runways or Instagram. Fashion is designed for the young; however, STYLE is for everyone.

From my perspective, EMBRACING my age means that I also embrace the times in which I live. I can't be in 2020 if everything is fully planted in the 1960s. Hairstyles, clothing, approach to life, the 'way things are done' all need to move with the times. It doesn't mean that I'm trying to be a thirty-something; it DOES mean that I incorporate new with tried-and-true (for me). My approach is to take elements of what's new and fold it into what works for me. Maybe it's this year's color (if it looks good on me), or it's finding a pencil skirt with the exposed zipper, or once again wearing tie-dye in a modern way. I do my hair, paint my nails, wear my high heels (because, for me, they are more comfortable than flats), blush on my cheeks, and strut my stuff, not for anyone else but me!

When I look in the mirror, I do see a few lines and grey curls, but that shows that I have lived a life, and no one can take those experiences (both good and bad) away from me. My style says I'm comfortable in my own skin and dare anyone to hide me in a corner. Being a bit braver than I thought I could be. Now THAT's sexy! Thank goodness, we bold ladies are seen in more places than just the ads for medicines or retirement communities.

We still have much to contribute to the world if we choose to do so. Embrace the age that you are! Remember, some folks never got to be this age. Think of the Red Hat Society ladies who continue to throw themselves into their worlds with joy in their hearts, laughter in their faces, color, and style in their dress, with new friends and goals on their horizons. I say, "Never give in, and never give up!" The sixties and beyond is our reality, and we should live it to the fullest.

Onward and upward, and full steam ahead!

*S*ylvia **Headen Douglin** has a enjoyed a thirty-year career as a Corporate Trainer providing training, facilitation and professional development to a wide range of Federal government and private sector customers. For the last twenty years she has worked in the hospitality industry holding roles of Director of Training for three top hotel companies where she is responsible for overseeing training design and delivery efforts for the company. She trains hospitality industry and corporate leaders to speak before clients and groups via effective presentation skills, workshops and individualized coaching sessions. She conducts Instructor Skills for aspiring trainers to deliver exceptional workshops that exceed customer expectations, participants' needs and adhere to company standards of excellence.

Sylvia began as a runway model in the greater Boston area in her early twenties when she was recruited by the John Powers Finishing and Modeling School as a modeling instructor. That experience was the start of her training career and evolved into Image Consulting for commercial and government entities and for private clients including television personalities, national motivational speakers, and business professionals. Runway modeling remained a large part of her life. During her modeling days, Sylvia worked runways in Boston, New York, Seattle, and Washington DC into her late 50's.

Based on these initial opportunities and experiences, she developed her signature program, "Image and Upward Mobility", that she currently delivers to businesses and colleges through her company ***Refined Training & Consulting (RT&C).***

Sylvia is also a prolific fashion designer. She was accepted at the Fashion Institute of Technology (FIT) in 1970 for both fashion design and fashion illustration. She has continued designing through the years and is currently focusing on a collection of coats.

Refined Training & Consulting is now the vehicle through which Sylvia runs her training and image consulting business. As a way to introduce emerging leaders, innovators, government and future entrepreneurs, RT&C delivers a program of "Professionalism" to matriculating college graduates and young professionals. This exclusive RT&C offering provides the participants with skills, information and an understanding of how initial images, workplace behaviors, workplace decisions and interactions, initiative and communication can impact first impressions and affect individual's reputations in the early days of their careers (or employment?) and beyond.

Rosetta Thompson, 62

SEXY: The Spirit
EXpresses ResiliencY

Rosetta Thompson

It came like a gushing wave over me. . . this awesome wonderment of excitement! I suddenly couldn't wait to be sixty! I had just turned fifty-nine, and never would I have thought that being sixty would be soooo exciting! I felt my life was beginning again for the third time!

The second time was when I had been born again at the age of twenty-one. I asked Jesus Christ to be my Lord and Savior. He's everything to me, more than a story. I couldn't tell my story without Him being in it. He IS my story! The Holy One, The Alpha and The Omega, The Beginning and The End, The Lord God Almighty! My life was reborn on a plane to a job interview in Minnesota in 1980. I didn't take that job, but accepted a better offer at IBM (International Business Machines) in Maryland. Everything that I had prayed for, I had received. I was like a child asking her Father, the Creator of the Universe, for a blessing which He was all too willing to grant, just like any earthly parent would. I had heard about His promises and that the Bible said you could have whatever you said: that you could ask, seek, and believe, *and so I did!* And God did! But as the years went on, I discovered that it wasn't that simple. At twenty-one, I was a baby all over again!

When you are a toddler, you are trained and disciplined to know better and then begin to do better. My parents laid a foundation of obedience, respect, and hard work, which had helped in my walk with The Lord. My life of receiving, being chastised, rewarded, pruned, blessed, and loved by my Heavenly Father, my Friend, and my God. I asked Him, "What should I write about?" Then, one of my favorite songs, 'My Story' by Big Daddy Weave, came on the radio (because that's how Abba Father rolls with me). There is a lyric in this song that says, "To tell you my story is to tell of Him." So, this is my story!

WHO HAVE I BEEN?

I'm a child, a friend, a teenager, employee, employer, CEO, entrepreneur, manager, caterer, baker, florist, wife, mother, teacher, artist, encourager, advisor, confidant, planner, mentor, author, a child of God and a student, which I will always be. At the heart of it, I have been an entrepreneur all of my life. This was all I was exposed to when I was growing up. It's no wonder this was my ultimate goal after college. I was born and raised in Baltimore City, the youngest of seven. My parents were entrepreneurs, although they were not called that back in those days. My Dad was a carpenter. He was very creative in styling and hand making furniture all by himself. My mother was a housekeeper; that is, she found her jobs by cleaning peoples' homes.

I have always been a risk-taker. I was the first of my family to go out-of-state to college, living on campus. Later, I chose to move to North Carolina (N.C.) at twenty-eight, not knowing anyone in the state, for another position in IBM. Some risks that I have taken did not pan out well; however, this one did. I was able to build best friend relationships and gain a whole new family of loving people who are still, to this day, praying for me to return 'back home'. In N.C., I decided to leave my job at IBM on an early 'out' to begin what I always wanted to do - become an entrepreneur in 1991. Sure, in taking risks, sometimes you don't know exactly what to do. Well, this time I really didn't know what to do, so I did it all! I had a business in catering, image consulting, job interviewing preparation, wardrobe consultation, and interior design! Even while working daily to grow the company, I learned that a successful business is one that has found its niche market.

WHERE HAVE I BEEN AND LIVED?

I did most of my traveling in the first thirty-five years of my life — traveling to many of the states within the continental United States, Hawaii, Panama, and many other islands. So, the more important question is, where has my life taken me?

I have been close to the mountaintop of success personally and in business. I have co-owned two brick and mortar businesses, several multi-level marketing business ventures, and in the mid-2000s, a Christian Coloring and Activity Book called "Fruitful Thoughts" that was available in several stores in the area. I also had a wonderful marriage for a while, living the American dream of having a husband, a house, a thriving business career, and a child. It was God's peace and my desire to close my business to be a stay-at-home mom for a while, when I homeschooled our daughter, Kayla. Then the dream crumbled; there was a divorce, and I was sent on a downward spiral. Many more heartaches, financial crises, transitions, bad decisions, and destitution followed. These valleys were deep, and my faith was shaken. I needed healing from the inside out. I felt lost, abandoned, and alone.

Oh, I had a lot of family and friends. I even went to a pretty good-sized church and was active there. However, when YOU are in the valley, sometimes it's too hard to look up. It hurts when you don't see anything familiar around you. When you're on your face while trying to get on your knees, you can't even see anyone who could even help you. It was then that my faith was tested to the max! It was then when God showed me, again, WHO He was! He gave me eleventh-hour faith, then 11:30 p.m. faith. After that, one time, I asked, "Where are you?" He didn't respond. I learned that my faith was being stretched yet again! He took me to 11:59 p.m. that time, but He did come through!

He is so faithful!

So again, where have I lived? I have lived through many tests and trials. So, for many decades and even now — I live at my spiritual address, Hebrews 13:5, "He will never leave you or forsake you."

WHAT HAVE I DONE?

I have, and still am, dreaming big! I have taken many, many risks! 'To get something you never had, you have to do something that you've never done.' I have failed, big and small. When I fell in the valley, though, I fell forward. Note to self: *always fall forward!* It's easier to get up on your knees and pray your way out. Fall forward on your faith, believing that you can get back up again and again, as many times as necessary. I have had successes, but success is no accident. It is hard work, perseverance, continuous learning, studying your craft, and sacrifice, but most importantly, loving what you are doing!

It warms my heart when I hear someone describe me, first, as a woman of faith. It lets me know that I am going in the right direction because without faith, you cannot please God. Those that come to Him must believe that He is and that He is a rewarder of those that diligently seek Him. So, I depend on God and not on my own strength, which is what He wants us to do. I only have one life to live, and I want it to point the way to Jesus. He changed my heart to love like He loves and uses my desires for His glory. He causes my desires to line up with His Word to lead people to Him. My faith is not based on my situation, but on my Savior; and the peace that I have is a peace that surpasses all understanding. However, whenever my faith is weak, He's right by my side, holding me up and pulling me through. When the going got tough, He showed up, moving, and working through people. His love has won me over, and He keeps pulling me closer.

MY HEALER, PROVIDER, AND MY PROTECTION

I experienced my first miracle at twenty-two. I was diagnosed with cervical cancer, Stage 3, heading for Stage 4. I was devastated! I left the doctor's office and drove straight home to my high-rise apartment in Rockville, Maryland. I didn't call or speak to anyone but God! I got to my bedroom, got on my knees, and began confessing every healing scripture that I knew, over and over again! That by the stripes of Jesus, I was healed. That I was covered in the blood of Jesus and as a child of God, total and complete healing was my birthright! I remember like it was yesterday. It was 5 p.m., and I was on my knees, praying, speaking in the Spirit, crying, and thanking my Heavenly Father for healing me. When I finally got up, I looked at my clock, and it was 8 p.m. I called my pastor of the church I attended then, Rhema Christian Center in D.C. (District of Columbia). As I told him what the doctor had said, what I believed, and what I had been doing for the past three hours, he began to agree with me in prayer.

As he was praying, my room began to get brighter and brighter and brighter. My eyes were still closed because I could NOT open them! It was like they were sealed. Then it happened, like something I had never felt before, or have ever been able to put into words to describe! Mere words are not adequate to describe the warmth, the security, the love that I felt from the top of my head to the bottom of my feet. It was thick like honey, warm like the sun, and gentle like a breeze. And then the light slowly left my room. My pastor finished his prayer. I told him what had happened, and confirming my miraculous healing, he said what Jesus said, "Go tell what God had done for me." I have ever since! First, at church, and then to the doctors, who couldn't explain what was no longer there. All praises to God!

Once, when I was a wounded Christian and needed a lot of healing, I couldn't even pray. I could only say, "Jesus, I need your help." God met me at my point of need and right where I was. He honored His Word and watched over His Word to perform it [Psalm 138:2; Jeremiah 1:12]. At my lowest point in 2009, He sent someone to help me in the mornings when I was getting myself and my daughter ready for the day. It was simply a morning prayer call that I made sure I was on each day. The host of the call did not realize that he was being used as my saving grace for those few months, and I didn't know until years later that I was the only person on the call. Those days, I was getting one dollar's worth of gas to get me from one job to the next, finding help wherever it came, because I couldn't see more than a foot in front of me. It was just God and me, and He pulled me up from the valley and restored my soul (Psalm 23:3). And that He did for me!

> *"Yea, though I walk through the valley of the shadow of death,*
> *I will fear no evil: for thou art with me; thy rod and thy staff they comfort me."*
> *-Psalm 23:4 (KJV)*

Many times, we think that we are getting through the days unscathed when it is God who is keeping us from harm. I learned back in the eighties, when I was a baby Christian, that the ninety-first Psalm is a Psalm of protection. I memorized the entire chapter by heart and still know it today.

I remember walking alone across Howard University's campus yard at night, during a season when there was a high rape alert; I wanted to get some fried chicken on Georgia Avenue. On the way back to my dorm, as I was saying the ninety-first Psalm out loud, there was a car approaching me that had four guys in it. They slowed down and got the shock of their lives. I am sure, to this day, that they remember what they saw. I know they saw my towering angels over me. Each one of the guys had their mouths dropped wide open as the car screeched away in a hurry! Ever since that day, I was assured of the divine protection that was my portion as a child of God! Other instances have continued to show themselves to me, even to this day!

SEXY SIXTIES

When you are in your sixties, you have to realize that you need to take care of yourself! I take supplements for what my body is lacking and certified cannabidiol for other issues. How do I know what is lacking? I get both blood tests and sensitivity tests so that I know what my body does or doesn't need.

Yes, I've had to cut out certain foods, but not the general ones that everyone cuts out. These are foods that my body doesn't like! That's why I said that I am a lifetime student! I also believe I have no allergies because I don't use toxic products in my home. I get my supplies - household and personal - products from my entrepreneurial daughter, which includes soaps, lotions, makeup, and nail polish! I only use soap and water on my face and wear makeup sparingly! I attempt to eat healthy eight to ninety percent of the time because I do enjoy fried chicken, my carrot cake, and crème brûlée on occasion!

You also need to take care of your mind! I make sure that I meditate on God's Word, and I have always tried to live with an attitude of gratitude. The Bible says to renew your mind! That means that your mind can be renewed! Those brain synapses can be regenerated. It is possible not to have negative thoughts and tendencies — replacing them with positive ones. It is possible to lose negativity when you don't use it! We all have heard, if you don't use it, you lose it!

I have realized that a lot of wisdom has been shared with me in my sixty-plus years, and I hope that I have been able to pass some along to you. I pray my story has given you hope, inspiration, and confidence to know that the One who created you has you in the palm of His hand, and He wants the best of everything for you. What I know is that without commitment, you'll never start, and without consistency, you'll never finish. Dreams without goals are dreams with disappointments, and your goals cannot be achieved. Therefore, take risks, YOU are worth it! The people's lives you will touch are worth it! Remember, failure is

part of success. Jesus wasn't received at home, so what makes you think that your home won't reject you too? Never settle for less because you deserve the best. Ask yourself, what defines you? Is it what you do or whose lives you've changed? Is it how successful you are or how you get there?

Thus far, my life has been great, good, bad, and ugly — as most of our lives are. I've discovered a lot about people, places, and things, but mostly about myself! I've carried others' secrets and inspired others' dreams. I've trusted, been used, misused, lied to, lied about, loved, lost, and hurt. But He's the God who has stayed and never left. There were times that I did move away from God, living life for myself, doing my own thing without regard to what I already knew to be the right thing. But He was right there when I came back. No matter what I do, nothing can separate my love for Him or His for me.

We've only just begun!

Ever since I was a little girl in Baltimore, I was taught much about cooking and became the family mac-n-cheese person! While living in NC, I decided to do what I've always loved, cooking. I had always dreamed of working for myself, like my parents did. I started a business in catering and streamlined it to cake decorating. When I moved back to Maryland, I got married and opened a storefront, The Party and Wedding Gallery. I added florals to my business and became a Certified Floral Designer in 2000, the year I gave birth to our daughter, Kayla Rosetta. During my time as CEO of my own business and the General Manager of that storefront, my partners and I provided space for 12 other vendors creating a very successful one-stop shop for over 6 years. We planned bridal shows at hotels, hosted in-house bridal fairs and planned events for hundreds of satisfied clients.

Owning your own business is a 24/7 venture. I was blessed to be able to do this early in my life before becoming a mother. Endurance, perseverance, consistency, pruning, growing, learning, failing, and succeeding were all valuable experiences. I gained priceless knowledge by enhancing my craft, networking, being mentored, intentionally knowing my competition and building relationships with people in my industry.

In 1980, I made the most important decision of my life and received Jesus as my Lord and Savior and am learning to become more like Him. Without this decision, my accomplishments would not have been as elevated, anointed and successful.

The business wisdom I have gained over the past 30 years adds to the excitement of this journey. I recently had the joy of planning my 60th birthday party and was tickled red (favorite color).

Contact RT Inspired Designs with your next idea!

—Rosetta Thompson

Linda Marshall, 64

LIFE LESSONS

Linda Marshall

There were ten of us — eight kids and two parents — and, although we moved from home to home every two years, we figured out how to stay together. While my grandparents, Albert and Carolina Burgess, shared their gift of aging gracefully with me, my father, Melvin Christian, taught me about youthfulness in laughing loudly and taking pride in being a parent. My mother, Mary Burgess Christian, taught me to dream big, love myself, and not let anyone place limitations on me.

Being the fifth child of eight gave me insight into what to expect in life at sixty and the bumps of not paying attention along the way. My story isn't all pretty, but it's real. I was a teenage parent; I was homeless, lived in the roughest neighborhoods, and raised three kids alone, and so much more. Yet, I made it through. As I embrace my sixties, this message is to help you push forward through life with joy. Life is joy!

BY THE TIME HE WAS SIXTY...

Life started pretty stable. We lived a comfortable life. My grandmother, mother, siblings, and I lived in a house built by my grandfather's hands in the early 1900s. My grandfather, Albert, passed away and received his wings before I was born. I never physically met him; however, the incredible stories of his accomplishments helped shape my character at an early age. Imagine raising a family in the early 1900s. During that time, there was a clear divide. Blacks were struggling for economic equality, racial discrimination, and segregation in school. Although my family was up against the same issues, my grandfather managed to find success through his hard work and good fortune. By the time he was sixty, he had managed to use his self-taught skills to build houses, own properties, and land in a small town in Martinsville, VA. He was well respected and had a street named after him, Burgess Lane. Despite how unfair the U.S. was towards black people, my grandfather's willpower taught me the importance of pushing through adversity and finding solutions.

IN HER SIXTIES

After my grandfather's death, everything fell on my grandmother, Carolina (we called her Jama). She was left to figure out how to maintain the house, pay the bills, prepare food, all while taking care of my mother and her seven grandkids. During my early years, my mother loved to go out at night to parties. She was an incredible dancer. She loved my siblings and me, but she was rarely home; it was as if the sound of the music and nightlife came and picked her up every night. So, in her sixties, my grandmother was left to raise her seven grandchildren.

My grandmother made sure our needs were met. We may not have had stylish clothes and the newest toys, but we had what we needed: a home, food, and love. My grandmother was an incredible cook. She learned to cook at a very young age. I was told that she cooked for a white man when she wasn't even tall enough to reach the stove. She used a stool to maneuver her way around the kitchen. You could smell the aroma from her food miles away. Her food fed your soul. With very little money, she opened her kitchen to anyone. I loved sitting and watching as my Jama prepared meals. I remember the first time she asked me to cook with her. It was peaceful. My siblings were outside playing, and I was learning recipes passed down for generations.

These were great memories and times that carry on in my heart. She taught me that family is important, and the role of a grandmother was truly special. Because of her, I utilize the kitchen as a bonding time with my children and grandchildren. Even as a young girl, I knew that I wanted to create an environment within my family like the one she had created for me.

MY FATHER

My mother and father moved us to Washington, D.C., when I was at the tender age of four. My father was a Navy man. Having him home helped fill part of the hole that I felt deep down in my heart when my grandmother received her wings. He was my hero. Some of the fun family times we had together were dancing, picnics, and trips to the beach in the summertime. The house was filled with laughter and love. My father's siblings lived in New York, and his mother lived in Norfolk, Virginia. That meant road trips. I can remember piling into my father's car and hitting the road at all times of the night, just my father and his younger children (myself and my three younger siblings) would go on these adventurous road tours. Did I say that there were eight children in total? There were four girls and four boys. I was the fifth child. During the road trip, when my father got tired, he pulled over onto the side of the road, so we could sleep until the sun came up. I can still hear the cars passing and crickets throughout the night; it was always a peaceful sleep — even in the midst of the chaos of our continuous moving. Money was tight, and there weren't many lessons he could teach us about finances, but he gave us the gift of unconditional love. My father loved his children, and the value of laughing and loving my kids, no matter what, has carried me throughout my life.

MY MOTHER

My mother is the strongest woman I know. My mother taught my brothers to hand dance and the girls to sew. By the time I was a teenager, my mother was a single parent. Her courage to raise both my older siblings and teenagers displayed her inner strength and her willpower to keep us all together.

Another lesson I learned from my mother is to envision what you want. If you want a house, see yourself in that house, with as many details as possible. You have to believe that you already have the house. Just like it says in the Bible, "Ask and it shall be given unto you" (Matt. 7:7 NIV). My mother also taught me how to pray. What I learned from my Mom has helped me my entire life and led me to a book called "The Secret," which is all about manifesting and believing you have what you want before you receive it. I always had the vision that I would have my life portrayed in a book one day, and now here we are... "I am in a book, Mom!"

She did everything she could to keep her eight children together, teaching us to always be there for one another, and just by being a strong, beautiful black woman. My mother was not the perfect mother, and neither was I, yet her lessons have guided me to the woman I am today.

A PIVOTAL MOMENT OF CHANGE

As I moved from early childhood into my teenage years, I found myself trying to figure out what it meant to be a teenager. I was the only sibling lacking self-confidence. I adored my sisters' beauty and brothers' charm, but I felt those genes skipped over me. I found myself in relationships that weren't healthy. I learned about boys and dating through my female friends, and I did as my girlfriends did — we dated the boys in the neighborhood. There were four boys and four girls, so the boys picked the girl they wanted, and that was our boyfriend. I only wanted to date one guy, but I guess my boyfriend had other ideas. He wanted me and someone else at the same time. It was not a healthy relationship. I continued a cycle of unhealthy relationships and became a teenage mother while in high school. How does a girl, coming to grips with her own identity, begin to raise another human being?

I could not be who I was with this child. My fear became my fuel, and my faith in GOD became stronger. I wasn't ready, but when my daughter, Nytika, was born, my life changed. There was so much that I had to learn and **fast**. My mother asked, "What are you going to do with a baby?" I replied, "Take care of her." And that is what I did. She was the most beautiful baby in the world. I looked at her and realized, to create something that beautiful, I had to be beautiful. I am beautiful.

I was eighteen with a newborn, unemployed, and determined. It was a struggle with little support. People stared in disgust as I breastfed my daughter while traveling to night school on the bus. Breastfeeding wasn't fashionable in the seventies. But at this point, I didn't care. Feeding my daughter and finishing school was more important to me than the opinions of others. I did not know how to care for an infant, but I learned one day at a time. I didn't know how I was going to finish school, but I figured it out. I finished night school and became a medical secretary.

FAST FORWARD

Over time, I was married for thirty years, had five children, fourteen grandchildren, and three great-grandkids. I also earned an Associate Degree, a Bachelor's Degree, a Master's Degree, and started my own business. It was a great accomplishment to be the first of my siblings to attend college and earn a degree, and the look of pride on my mother's face as I walked across the stage to receive my degree, melted my heart. I had worked hard and done my best to set good examples for my children — demonstrating the importance of working toward their goals. Today, two of my girls have earned Bachelor's Degrees, the other two girls have their Master's, one has her own business, and my only son is an active member of the U.S. Army.

However, the good news is that I did not do it alone — my husband, who has been in this for thirty years, worked alongside me to ensure that our children had what they needed — even if they didn't always get what they wanted. Now, I'm genuinely proud of my family for what they have achieved. Raising my kids has taught me how capable I truly am — loving someone more than yourself will have you become more than you would be by yourself. A lesson I learned from my mother was "never give up"; therefore, one thing I have done well is that I have never given up on my family — or myself.

My incredible children have blessed me with amazing grandchildren; every moment with my grandchildren is special to me, and as I watch my children raise their children, it brings me joy that they have instilled some of the core values I am sharing with you through my story. I look forward to watching my grandchildren and great-grandchildren grow.

EMBRACING MY SEXY SIXTIES

I began to embrace my sexy sixties through a reflection of the many things I have prevailed through and looking at my beauty through my own lenses versus the lenses of those around me. I now understand that life is about learning through your pain, taking each experience, and using it to become better. Today, I stand here a proud, beautiful black woman using all of the lessons I have learned throughout my life, finally comfortable in my skin. I am victorious, and the insecure young girl is now a confident matriarch of a family. I can look toward the future, knowing that the rest of my life will be the best of my life, and as I embrace my sexy sixties, I realize, even more, how truly blessed I am.

While I was not a perfect parent, my struggles and victories have taught my children how to be better parents. I have spent the last six decades going to school to better myself and to provide for my family. Now it's time for me to get to know me on a deeper level. I'm reading more self-help books and doing a lot of self-reflection. I'm changing from needing to please everyone to doing what makes Linda happy.

One definition of sexy is exciting, and as I look back at old pictures, I recognize that I was *beautiful*. So, as I embrace my sexy sixties, I embrace the reality that I am still beautiful — and it is exciting. My style has transformed into a more mature and sexier look because I am now free to be sixty and sexy. I invest in my health through diet and exercise, not to look perfect, but to feel confident in my skin. I also drink plenty of water, make homemade meals, and get plenty of rest. Most importantly, I laugh often.

NOTE TO SELF

If given the opportunity, what would I tell my younger self? I would tell her: *You got this! Your brown skin and hair are gorgeous. Don't let other people define you. Most people are immature and don't know true beauty. I know you are scared, and your biggest concern is how you will take care of your baby. You got this. Your belief in a Higher Power and perseverance will propel you forward. You have five beautiful kids, and you are married to an incredible man. You have traveled the world, you have your own home-based business, and you give back to single parents. I am proud of you, Smart, Beautiful, and Sexy Black Woman. Continue to be you.*

WHAT'S NEXT?

After I retire from my career, I plan to become a Licensed Social Worker and a Licensed Christian Counselor. I'm excited about taking the courses and tests to earn my Social Worker license and opening a Christian Counseling Service Center. There have been several times throughout my life when I needed counseling support, and it was challenging to find a Christian Counselor; only a few churches have the resources, so I want to provide this much-needed service.

I also desire to create a foundation for breastfeeding and continue a legacy my mother started by donating breast pumps to as many mothers as possible. See, my mother breastfed all eight of her children, passing its importance to her children, and we continue to pass it on to ours. Although breastfeeding is more acceptable today than when I was raising my children, young women still need to understand the benefits. That is why it is my goal to provide pumps to those in need — wherever the need.

Personally, I want to travel internationally every three months. I have been told there are beaches with red, white, and black sand; there are beaches with pink water. Imagine that! So, I want to visit beaches all over the world. While I am at it, I believe I could also learn how to swim. I never learned, and now is a good time. It would be an incredible experience to swim in the different bodies of water all around the world. I'm not sure if I will swim in the pink water, but I would definitely love to feel it touching my toes!

Listen, continuing to learn and grow is based on willpower —not age. So, remember, it's not how you start; it's how you finish that matters most. Although my beginnings were not a fairytale, I have no regrets. My sixties, on the other hand, the world is *not* ready.

I have embraced my Sexy Sixties, and I am excited about it!

*L*inda Marshall believes the key to success is discovering not only your calling but how to use it in the service of others. As a Family Engagement Specialist with the United Planning Organization, she works with families in the Head Start Program, which works with low-income parents to reach their goals. To expand her calling, Linda's business, Team International Revolution, provides essential services to help people create generational wealth.

Her calling was dictated by her education: Medical Secretary- B.S. Social Work and M.S. Christian Counseling. Linda also holds a Social Worker, Doula, and Christian Counselor and family Development Credential. Mental Health First Aid from the Department of Missouri Mental Health and Infant Massage Certificate from Infant Massage USA and a Reiki Master in June of 2019.

Linda's motto is that you make a living by what you get, but you make a life by what you give. She knows that volunteers do not necessarily have the time, they just have the heart, and she does. Her volunteer efforts include Mt. Jezreel Baptist Church: Christian Counseling; The Questers Inc, providing 4-year college scholarships; and Sister 4 Sisters Network Inc (S4SN), focused on domestic violence and mental health issues.

Even with her busy schedule, Linda's devotion belongs to her family. The daughter of Melvin & Mary Burgess Christian, Linda, is also the wife of Guy Marshall for 31 years. Added to this union are four daughters, one son, 14 grandchildren, and two great-grandchildren.

Linda believes that her best life is yet to come. She wants to work with pregnant women; mothers when they are in most need of help. The goal is to start a foundation to provide breast pumps for mothers in need. She knows that God will not give her more than she can handle.

Angela C. Gaither-Scott, 67

SMALL TOWN GIRL TAKING OVER THE WORLD

Angela C. Gaither-Scott

I grew up in a small neighborhood in Glen Burnie, MD. It had a small community church, including many of my relatives, and our house was always filled with family and friends; we were truly a village that looked out for each other. I was fortunate to be one of thirteen children, so I was protected by my brothers and sisters, my teachers, *and* the community. There were also many times that our home was filled with not only my siblings, but many of their friends; life was always fun and eventful when we celebrated holidays with large dinners, cookouts, and beach parties.

The house we lived in sat on a small farm where my father grew produce, and my mother was the consummate homemaker. I was bussed to an all-black, Harman Elementary School that was over eight miles from my home. All my teachers were friends of my family; we lived in a segregated area where many people of color knew each other. I remember when my brother had appendicitis; his teacher visited the house to check on him. Mrs. Wade, my fifth-grade teacher, and I frequently talked and went out to lunch regularly. I was blessed with teachers who not only took a personal interest in students, but made certain to prepare us to compete educationally. I will never forget that day in middle school when I realized that I was more prepared than most other students who had attended predominately white schools in the area. Looking back on those days, it feels warm to have grown up in such a loving environment.

I really don't remember having any catastrophic events until I lost my brother, Gerald. He was killed in a car accident before his twenty-first birthday. He had attended a trade school and enlisted in the Army. I remember how sad I was, watching him pack his duffle bag in anticipation of leaving for boot camp. I always emulated him. He played in the band, so I played in the band. We both had gaps in our front teeth. I just knew we would always be together. The night of the accident, my father went to the hospital. When he came home, he avoided answering my mother's demands. When he finally told her that Gerald didn't survive the accident, our world was never the same. I knew I could react to this news negatively or positively. I decided that my brother would have wanted me to succeed and always put my best foot forward. So, I chose to excel in everything I did. Somehow, I felt him looking down on me and smiling. Keeping this in my head helped me cope with his loss.

When it was time for me to attend middle and high school, I looked forward to enrolling in the same Bates Middle and Bates High Schools my siblings had attended, between the sixth to twelfth grades. Unfortunately, it was decided that desegregation in Anne Arundel County would be enforced, so I would be going to Corkran Middle and Glen Burnie High Schools. Naturally, I had all types of preconceived ideas about how I would fit in. I had always been a popular girl in my elementary school. I remember the first day of middle school; I was asked about another student with the last name of Gaither. I found out later that she was white, which meant she was part of my family that had mixed decades ago. She and I never spoke about that.

I was determined to continue the activities that I had started. So, I was in the band and served as a student government representative. I was surprised to find out that I knew more than most of my classmates. I always made A's but never got recognized. One of my teachers told me he had nominated me for the National Honor Society. He felt I deserved it, but of course, he was only one person. I soon realized that the nurturing experiences I had received in elementary school had not followed me; I was constantly reminded that I didn't belong. I remember how many teachers made the black students sit in the back of the class and consistently admonished them for talking to each other.

One instance that stands out in my mind was when I had received all A's and one B in French. I remember telling my mother that I had earned all A's that marking period. When I met with my French teacher to inquire as to why she had given me a B, she informed me that I did not participate in class. Of course, I reminded her that I had raised my hand numerous times, only to be passed over to hear a white student stumble to answer the question. It didn't matter to her that I had received all A's on my tests and quizzes. I had never talked back to a teacher, but I argued that I thought she was unfair. After that day, she never even looked in my direction when we were in class. Still, I showed up to class and continued to put in my best effort; I was determined that this teacher was not going to discourage me from learning all I could.

When it was time to enter the ninth grade, I attended Glen Burnie High School. By that time, I had made acquaintances and soon discovered that the teachers were the ones who had a problem with integration.

I continued my involvement in the marching band and the student government. What was monumental was being one of the first blacks to be chosen for the homecoming court and to run for Miss Glen Burnie High. I will never forget stressing over being picked up to ride in the Homecoming parade. One of my classmates came to pick me up in a Cadillac convertible, and I rode in the parade, waiving like I was a princess. At the time, I didn't realize that I was making history. When it was time to graduate, we met with our school counselor. Even though I was graduating with honors, the counselor recommended that I attend a community college before transferring to a four-year university. I never said anything, but I knew I was ready for college and completely ignored that advice. Situations like this helped me decide to be the first in my family to attend college. I will never forget how proud my parents were when I got accepted at so many colleges. My mother was only able to complete the fourth grade because her father didn't think girls needed an education. My father told us how he traveled by train from Glen Burnie to Baltimore to attend Douglass High School. He would have loved to go to college, but he didn't have the means. The day my parents took me to college was a red-letter day in my family.

Even though I thrived in the desegregated schools, I decided that I wanted to attend a Historically Black College or University (HBCU). That's when I decided to enroll in Morgan State College (now Morgan State University). These were the best four years of my life. I got on campus and saw so many successful black educators. I was so inspired to do my very best. My first professor, Dr. Bernie Hollis, was my English instructor. He made writing fun and interesting. I was approached by so many students to join organizations. I wasn't familiar with fraternities and sororities, but I was intrigued. Looking from the outside, it seemed that they were having all of the fun. When I entered Morgan, I had no idea what fraternities and sororities did. I went to step shows and saw the Greek symbols and colors. I was most impressed by the closeness of its members. After observing the different sororities, I decided I wanted to be a Delta.

In my sophomore year, I decided to interview for a sorority. I thought it might be fun to see how the interviews were conducted. When I got the letter asking me to join, I was surprised. Along with twenty other progressive women, I became a member of Delta Sigma Theta Sorority, Inc. I was the president of my line, and then, the president of the Alpha Gamma Chapter, where I formed a special connection with my sorority sisters and an even stronger bond with the sisters that pledged with me. Even after forty-nine years, I am still in contact with many of them. We travel together, attend functions, and talk frequently. I have continued my sisterhood in the Baltimore County Alumnae chapter because of the value I place on the volunteer activities that my sorority provides for the community, and I'm excited about celebrating my golden anniversary in 2021.

I will always remember my days at Morgan State University with fondness. I had the pleasure of serving as vice president of my senior class. Many of my classmates are still in touch. Even though I was excited to graduate, it was a sad day because I knew I would never see many of them after graduation. The class of 1974 has celebrated many anniversaries together; I look forward to seeing them at Homecoming, Alumni luncheons, and special events. It is always heartwarming to catch up with each member. Unfortunately, we have lost many of our classmates. This serves as a reminder that we should fulfill our dreams and goals without reservations.

After graduating from Morgan, I started my teaching career; however, I soon realized that I had not yet found my calling. That's when I began my quest to find the perfect career. Growing up, I had no idea what I wanted to do. In addition to my parents, my role models were my elementary school teachers, of which many were my neighbors. I majored in Elementary Education and taught for ten years. I decided that I needed a change and found computers interesting. So, I went back to school to learn how to fix computers. Little did I know that at the time, this was a male-dominated profession! This made me more determined to succeed. After only five years, I was promoted to manager of twenty-five men. During this time, I also sold real estate. Soon after, I was approached by my manager to take a job as a systems analyst, which meant traveling to New Jersey during the week, until the office moved to Maryland. I didn't have the foggiest idea of how to help customers with their software, but I was determined to get the job. So, I purchased Microsoft Office and loaded it onto my computer. I spent the entire weekend teaching myself how to maneuver through Word, Excel, PowerPoint, and Access. By Monday, I went into the interview and convinced them that I was ready to be a Systems Analyst.

Before long, I was encouraged to go back to school to get my master's degree. I decided to get my Master's in Information Systems and Telecommunications at Johns Hopkins University. I was so glad that I made this decision because my systems analyst job transferred to Atlanta. This degree qualified me to get a job at Lucent Technologies, where I was the program manager for the Retrofit Program — the program that installed ATMs on Navy ships. Unfortunately, this job only lasted about five years because the Telecom industry bottomed out. Of course, this meant I needed to find a new career.

That's when I found my niche in the Financial Advisor industry. I secured my insurance and securities licenses. I was able to assist many customers with preparing for catastrophic events by purchasing life insurance and setting up investment plans. This was one of the most rewarding career paths because I was able to educate and help so many people. I was also able to travel with this new profession, as a result of achieving levels in the business. After about six years, I was ready to try something new. By now, you've probably figured out that I like to try new things.

During all of these years, I always found a way to give back to my Alma Mater. I volunteered to work on the Morgan State University Gala committee. Each year, the MSU Foundation has a gala the night before the Homecoming game. We raise money to help students who need financial assistance to stay in school. In all of the years that I volunteered, I never thought about working at Morgan.

While out for a walk one day, I overheard someone talking about working at Coppin State University. I thought to myself, that sounds like something I should explore. I contacted a friend I knew that worked there and asked if I could come in to talk to her — I was hired to recruit for the School of Education and eventually began advising students. While working at Coppin, I was able to complete an articulation agreement to bring in students who wanted to major in education. I was so proud to be a part of expanding the Education program.

When a position at Morgan, in the Office of Retention, became available, I applied. I came in as an advisor in the College of Liberal Arts. I was promoted to Retention Coordinator for the School of Community Health and Policy. It is so rewarding to help incoming freshmen navigate their first year in college. I now work as a Retention Specialist, where I assist students with scholarship opportunities and advise them on what is necessary to complete their education.

One of my most significant accomplishments has been forming a Morgan State Alumni Chapter of over four hundred members. To date, our RED Dynasty MSU Alumni Chapter is the largest alumni chapter at Morgan. We have raised over $120,000 through our RED Dynasty Endowment Fund. As a result of our success, the founding members of the chapter received the coveted 2017 Special Achievement Award from the Morgan State University Alumni Association. As the chapter president, I am so proud of our members. I have called on them numerous times to help students, and they always are willing to give their time, talents, and money.

I have had many careers – teacher, computer technician, systems analyst, real estate agent, financial analyst – but working with students has been my most rewarding. Even though I have explored many careers, my secret passion is to one day write a book. For now, being a member of the *More Than a Book Club* and participating as a contributing author within this book, may be the next best thing.

I was fortunate to have two daughters who, like me, value the importance of education. My oldest daughter, Dominique, graduated from North Carolina A & T and Stevenson University. My youngest daughter, Morgan, graduated from Salisbury University. I'm happy to say they are both gainfully employed and prospering. I am also delighted to be a new grandmother; my daughter, Dominique, has a son named Mason, and he is the light of my life. I believe it is so important to pass on the positive values that were instilled in me. My father taught me the importance of determination. My mother always emphasized compassion and devotion. Being a member of a family that included twelve siblings, I certainly had to learn to share and be patient.

Hearing stories from my family, I always thought I should write a book. My father used to talk about his mother being the first black teacher in Anne Arundel County, MD. I enjoyed writing when I was in school, but for some reason, I never found the time to transfer this story from my head to paper. I could also write a book about growing up during desegregation and how I was able to cope with all of the challenges.

My sister always talks about being a direct descendant of Charles Carroll, who was the last person to sign the Declaration of Independence. I have so many stories to explore.

I had other plans for my sixties. By now, I thought I would be retired, with my house paid in full, and traveling to all parts of the world. Instead, at the age of sixty, I find myself a single person who is loving life. Having been married for over thirty years, I was not sure how I would feel as a single woman. In the past few years, I have changed jobs and moved to a new area. I recently decided to purchase another home. My focus, now, is to make sure my grandson is given all of the opportunities that help him grow to be a fulfilled young man. In addition, my current goals are to do more traveling because I genuinely enjoy meeting new people and experiencing other cultures.

When I look back at my life, I must say that it has been very fulfilling. So, rather than looking at this season as the latter part of my life, I choose to look at it as a new beginning. I am embracing my sixties with enthusiasm and vitality – I am ready to try new adventures, like writing my book in the near future. Therefore, I say, bring on my seventies, eighties, nineties, and beyond; age is only a number, and it's how you feel that makes all the difference.

My ultimate goal is to make each day count. My next years will be my best years.

Bring it on, world!

*A*ngela C. Gaither-Scott graduated from Morgan State University with a Bachelor of Science degree in Elementary Education. She received a Master of Science in Information Systems and Telecommunication from Johns Hopkins University. She developed a passion for education while teaching elementary school students in the Baltimore City Public Schools. Angela has engaged in several careers. She has worked as a Project Manager, a Systems Analyst, a Real Estate Agent and a Financial Planner. She used her career changes as an opportunity to grow. Her current position is at Morgan State University. As the Retention Coordinator for the School of Community Health and Policy and College of Liberal Arts, Angela was responsible for assisting with the coordination of the overall student retention activities. Her current position of Student Scholars and Strategic Partners Specialist gives her the opportunity to assist student scholars to successfully complete matriculation at Morgan. Angela's goal is to develop ongoing relationships with the students that not only enriches their knowledge base but also encourages them to succeed in their chosen profession. As an alumnus of Morgan State University, she is committed to giving back to the university. Angela is a Diamond Life member of Delta Sigma Theta Sorority, a public service organization. She has been an active member of the Morgan State University Gala Committee for over twenty-five years. She is a life member of the Morgan State University Alumni Association. In addition to being a member of the MSU Howard County Alumni Chapter, Angela is the president of the newly chartered RED Dynasty MSU Alumni Chapter and a Life Member of the MSU Alumni Association. She received the 2017 Special Achievement Award for chartering the largest alumni chapter of 400 members at MSU and raising over $100,000 for the RED Dynasty MSU Endowment. Angela is the proud mother of two daughters, Dominique and Morgan and grandmother to Mason.

Betty Entzminger, 62

MANIFESTING B'S JOURNEY

Betty Entzminger

When you are down to nothing, God is always up to something…
God sees you, knows where you are, and can put His
hands on you in the twinkling of an eye!

As I consider my path through this amazing journey, I have gained a greater appreciation for my opening quote. I've discovered that God is aware of my every move because I am, now, and always have been, securely seated in the hollow of His hand. He designed my path, plotted my course, and He orchestrates my steps so that every step brings me closer to manifesting His plan for my life.

I am Betty Spriggs Entzminger, born the ninth of ten children to my phenomenal parents, Raymond and Mildred Spriggs. I am a native Washingtonian, a mother of two incredibly beautiful daughters, and the proud Nanaboo/Grandmother to my precious grandson. I was born in North East, D.C., now called Capitol Hill, a community vested in historical landmarks and strength, with ancestral purpose. I did not grow up with a silver spoon, as some might say, but I was taught strong values by a mother who was deeply rooted in God. Her philosophy and favorite scripture, respectively are "*God can do anything but fail,*" and "*You have not, because you ask not.*" *(James 4:6 AKJV)* When you trust Him, your values extend beyond material possessions and accolades.

Those little nuggets right there have sustained me through my most difficult and challenging times. So, please allow me to give you a glimpse of my journey…

NEIGHBORHOOD LANDMARKS WHERE WE PLAYED

Strict instructions to stay in our own neighborhood and return home when the streetlights came on — or a spanking would be waiting for you — limited our movement to explore other neighborhoods and kept us from venturing too far away. I did not want a spanking; therefore, I adhered to my mother's rules (although I strayed a couple of times). These are the landmarks that helped to forge a strong sense of community and culture for me.

Lincoln Park

Lincoln Park is where the Mary McLeod Bethune statue stands, strategically positioned at the southeast end of the park's play area. Mary McLeod Bethune, with the two children perched by her side, represented guidance, presence, and accomplishments. Her work and legacy were pivotal reminders to stay in school and manifest greatness. How grateful I am to have grown up in a community entrenched with such a rich black history.

Robert F. Kennedy Memorial Stadium

The Robert F. Kennedy Memorial Stadium is historic within its own right, a landmark that shaped my perspective of the community. At one point, there was nothing there but water, so when the area evolved, it was fascinating to see the stadium built for everyone's enjoyment. My siblings and I enjoyed free concerts, free games, and the circus there.

The Car Barn

The Car Barn is on East Capitol Street N.E. and was where the old trains parked their dilapidated cars. However, for us, it offered our creative minds the freedom to explore as far as our imaginations would take us. Now the Car Barn is a development infused with beautiful townhomes, condominiums, and exquisite landscapes — leaving only a remnant of what used to be.

DISTRICT OF COLUMBIA PUBLIC SCHOOLS

I attended these District of Columbia Public Schools: Maury Elementary, Eliot Junior High, and then the famous Eastern Senior High School, and I had the pleasure of performing at Duke Ellington School of the Arts. I have so many fond memories because my ancestors paved the way so that we could have the privilege of attending these prominent schools. God placed some beautiful jewels along my path to help me navigate my way. They helped me to develop many of my best qualities and to discover and nurture many of my gifts and talents. Even though I did not fully understand it all then, I certainly do now. So, let me share some experiences that, even now, make me gleam just to recall and write about them.

Visualize with me for a moment, if you will…

Maury Elementary School

Maury Elementary is the same school that all of my siblings attended, and as the ninth child, I had no choice but to follow their example. Here's a funny story: In the first grade, I got a brand-new pink sweater that I was so proud to wear to school. On that particular day, a classmate and I were called to the blackboard to solve a problem. However, my classmate took the eraser and hit my brand-new sweater. *Oh no*, I thought, *my mother is going to be mad at* me, and I sure did not want to make her angry. But before I could hit my friend back, the teacher interrupted us and made both of us sit down. Fortunately, I did not get into trouble when I got home. I was happy with that outcome, but I was still mad at my friend. Until one day, she wore something new, and I did the exact same thing to her! We were silly little girls who grew up to become lifetime Best Friends Forever.

My Jewels

Mrs. Adams was our Principal, one whom we all adored. Ms. Dorsey, the school librarian, stood out because I fell in love with books at an early age; she always let me stay in the library longer than the other children to explore books and to help her — until one of the other children got on her last nerve, then we all had to leave. I found a report card from the second grade, and there was a note to my mother that said, "*Please help Mildred (my former name) stay focused or she will have to repeat the **Second Grade**.*" WHAT! That is probably why I do not remember *that* teacher's name.

Nevertheless, how could I not mention Ms. Posey, the Music teacher. I started singing at the tender age of three, but outside of the church, no one had ever heard my voice, except for Ms. Posey. Thanks to her, I had so much fun discovering that my voice was an instrument. She made it comfortable for me to share my voice, as I was an unbelievably shy little girl with insecurities that manifested in ways that were very unattractive.

These three women left an inevitable imprint that I still vividly remember. I remember their greatness, their words of encouragement, and the precious time they invested in me.

Eliot Junior High School

My homeroom teacher was Mr. Ricks, and I was super excited to have him for homeroom. He was a funny adult with a childlike behavior at times, which made it easy for me to communicate with him openly. Mr. Ricks helped me overcome many insecurities and gave all of us privileges at times when we should have had none. *Mr. Ricks, you will forever be a person that I will honor on any platform when expressing acknowledgments of overcoming life challenges.*

Mr. Rhinehart taught Science. He made it so easy and engaging that it did not feel like the subject I had previously failed. I was eager to learn and discover more about space and the hemisphere through his creative way of connecting with youth. *Mr. Rhinehart, your teaching helped me to understand that we all do not teach or learn the same, but if you stay the course, you will get it by repetition. Thank you for never giving up on me.*

Mr. Hankerson taught History, a subject I vowed never to take again after his stern way of teaching. Mr. Hankerson's method of teaching History from the 1800's, and his insightfulness to infuse personal experiences, making it relevant to a room filled with inner-city kids, made him stand out as a great storyteller and a favorite teacher after all.

I actually began to encourage other children to take his class. *Mr. Hankerson, you would be extremely proud to know that understanding History and culture has kept me grounded in who I am, and I have become a better human being because of it.*

Eastern Senior High School

My five role models and motivators while at Eastern Senior High were Ma Nance, Ms. Dodd, Ms. Dennis, Ms. Coffee, Mrs. Garrett, and Our Beloved, Principal Sanders. I had so many great experiences, but I'll just highlight a few.

Ma Nance had been a staple at Eastern throughout my siblings' and my attendance. Her infamous quote, *"Eastern Is Proud"* is synonymous with her name. Ma Nance coordinated the entire cadre of events at Eastern, with the exception of the Music and Dance. Ma Nance is truly the definition of a Renaissance Woman who loved nurturing and helping others shine.

It was an honor to have auditioned and earned a chance to dance for the International Dance Troupe under the guidance of our premier ballerina teacher, Ms. Barbara Dodd. So much so, I decided that I wanted to be a premier ballerina. Sadly, my classmates conveyed to me that I was too tall to dance, which shattered my 'ballerina' belief, so I stopped dancing.

Ms. Dennis taught Gymnastics. I followed my friends to take her class, only to discover that this, too, was not for me. However, while in this class, her motivation is what stood out and kept me attending, even though my gymnastic skills were limited. When I completed this class, the motivation I came away with was always 'protect your mind, body, and stay agile'.

Ms. Coffee exuded grace and beauty with presence and strength in her business class.In the seventies, it was not always fashionable to wear an afro, and cultural garments, which was her style, yet she wore them boldly. She did not allow herself to be defined by others' opinions of her. What mattered to her was how she was going to influence a classroom of rambunctious young adults, waiting to understand business and its impact on our lives. She helped us to understand ownership, and taught us that, until we owned something, our freedom would always be in limbo. I will always appreciate the lessons imparted to me through her teaching, and her example of being a dynamic black woman.

Mrs. Joyce Garrett , the incomparable Choir teacher, was a beacon of light for all of us who were from single-parent households, because she became our second mother. Mrs. Garrett offered unlimited possibilities to dream as I never had before. She was the writer, director, composer, and producer of the musical "*I Gotta Keep Moving*," and my world exploded when she selected me to be in this renowned choir and complimented me on my musical gift. My singing gift had remained fairly hidden, even though I sang with our family gospel group, the Spriggs Singers, but now at the high school level, to be told that my gift was going to be seen by a new audience, sparked my excitement and I readily anticipated what was next.

Eastern High School was definitely where my talents blossomed. Ms. Garrett's musical was my first such performance — I played the role of Billie Holiday (gardenia in my hair and all). What a pivotal moment in the life of a growing young woman with a super big imagination. *Mrs. Garrett, you will always be a long-lasting treasure in my life, and I am eternally grateful to have learned so much from your tutelage.*

Duke Ellington School of the Arts became my dream high school before Eastern, but, being one of ten children did not afford me the opportunity to do so.

In my senior year, I became pregnant, and after graduating from Eastern High School, I auditioned for Street Theater Duke Ellington Summer Performing Arts Program, for the play called *Singing and Shouting*, and Producer/Director Mike Malone selected me. I learned, as a young single parent, that when you commit to your craft, the rewards will come. I met Debbie Allen that summer while performing with this arts program outside of The Lincoln Center in New York City — what a riveting experience this was! It gave me a positive spark because I had no clear-cut plans for my future.

The movie *Lean on Me* was a true example of who Principal Sanders was for us. 'Going Beyond' are the words stamped in my mind for him. *'Rest in Principalship', Sir, you have changed lives — one student at a time — and I am here as an example of the excellent work you have done.*

AN ARTISTIC CAREER PATH

Modeling

My mother and other family members often complimented my unique beauty as a gift from God and said I should always be grateful to have such features. They encouraged me to seek a career in modeling or in the field of entertainment, so I followed their advice. After high school, I pursued a career in modeling. I started out doing hair shows and moved into fashion, and eventually, runway and print modeling, affording me the opportunity to be a featured model in the internationally known Essence Magazine, Brides for Today Magazine, AARP Magazine and on the cover of New Homes Guide, New Luxury Estate Homes in Virginia and Maryland.

The Actress

I was on the path of modeling and enjoying it; however, after thirty-six plus years of modeling, I landed my first acting opportunity in *The Colored Museum,* under the direction of Professor Amelia Gray at the University of the District of Columbia. I was cast for the leading role as the understudy; however, I must admit, my respect for the craft was less than stellar. It was not until the second casting that I took acting seriously. My fellow actors lost their way on stage, so I started singing to end the scene. After that experience, I became entrenched in understanding the importance of learning lines and being committed to the work. Gratefully, since that time, I was cast in *In the Line of Fire, Black Body, I Don't, and Bride Price,* just to name a few. Recently, I was the understudy for Melba Moore in *The Home*, a play about Senior Care. It is always rewarding when I can sing and act in any production; it truly is a double benefit for me. My acting journey continues, and I anticipate many more blessings manifesting soon.

Singing

My family lineage has a long history of ministers, so it was inevitable to be a gospel singer, but jazz is my forte as well. While playing Billie Holiday, I became smitten with jazz. I had the wonderful opportunity to take vocal lessons from renowned vocal coach, Mr. Eddie Jackson. His ability to expand, stretch, and enhance your vocals sets him apart. Because of his God-given gift, I am now a mezzo vocalist.

OVERCOMING THE CHALLENGES

My most challenging life moment happened on October 1, 2014. The loss of my job created a domino effect, and after living in my apartment for well over sixteen years where long-term relationships were fostered, my daughters and I were evicted. I will never forget the sense of loss and failure I felt. I was so traumatized that I could not see past the pain that consumed me. Losing my job, becoming homeless, then having my possessions auctioned from the storage facility left me devastated. However, this experience helped me to do some deep soul searching. God has a way of getting our attention when we think we are in control, but our life is spinning out of control. I eventually realized enough is enough; so, I evicted pride and ego and fully surrendered to God.

THAT WAS THEN. THIS IS NOW

The manifestation of blessings began to unfold immediately. My life is by no means problem-free because challenges are a part of this journey, but my blessings overshadow my battles by far. There is simply not enough time or space to list, let alone expound on every encounter and adventure I've experienced on this journey so far, and my journey is not over! So, let me share some of the blessings that are manifesting in my 'now':

- **College graduate**: I am the first of my siblings to graduate college – University of the District of Columbia, 2016-2018, making the Dean's list and obtaining the Myrtilla Miner Humanitarian & Civic award.
- **Beneath the Crown**: Crowned American Classic Woman of the Year – awarded to women fifty-five years and older – July 2018 (escorted by my grandson).
- **Bold Brave & Beautiful**: Received the Unbreakable Spirit Award – 2019.

I leave you with these thoughts: This has truly been a journey of gratitude and of experiencing incredible miracle after miracle. One thing's for sure, I will always remember that it is because of God's Grace and Mercy that I made it through to write my story. Ephesians 5:15-16 became my roadmap, as I believe God's plan is that *"He may be most glorified in us, through us being satisfied in Him..."*

If we follow the path God has for us, God will be glorified, and we will walk confidently, knowing there is a power bigger, stronger, and greater than us working on your behalf. Being sexy at sixty is not about exterior beauty, but internal fortitude and endurance. I found that many became enamored with my outer beauty, but never took the time to embrace the beauty of my soul.

To them, I say:

> *[I am] educated, deep, witty, simple and young-hearted. I am naturally beautiful, honest, brave, loyal, and nurturing. I am the whole package — balanced, quirky, open-minded, complex, and flawed. I can be raw with my words, and gentle with my touch. I am soulful, connected and driven.*
>
> *-the betty sutras, June 24, 2013, Urban Dictionary (modified)*

Inspiring others should be the sole focus of Sexy at Sixty, motivating them to overcome obstacles and to come out of dark places; it is the blueprint to show the world how to live life with more zest and zeal. *Emerging from the ashes of obscurity, I rise — tall and talented, bald and brave, chosen and courageous; at age sixty-two, I am "B" . . . and this is my journey.*

BETTY ENTZMINGER

Model, Actor & Singer in Washington, DC

At a glance, Betty Entzminger's beauty and spiritual essence brings to mind both the intriguing mystic of Grace Jones and the sheer elegance of Dionne Warwick. However, upon closer view; as you watch her stride the length of a runway; or capture the uniqueness of her character; or, present a classical gospel spiritual you will discover Betty E's aura is exclusively her own.

Betty E's modeling credits are documented nationally. She is recognized as having graced the pages of Essence, Brides For Today, along with several other publications. She is, and perhaps will always be, the preferred model by top designers of Afro-centric Wear, throughout the United States...Having just the "right stuff," which she terms her "secret weapon" only serves to enhance the display of the garments and accessories in ways it really needs to be shown. To know Betty E is to be inspired by her inimitable African-ness...

Betty E's beauty, charm, grace, and poise are present in all characters she portrays. her acting resume' includes; The Colored Museum, In The Line of Fire, For The Colored Girls Who Have Considered Suicide When the Rainbow Is Enuf, and Don't Sing No Blues For Me...partial listing.

Betty E's singing talents began early in her childhood. As the daughter of a Baptist Minister, her musical talents blossomed in the Churches of Washington, DC. Her passion for singing continues to overwhelm the hearts of thousands, whenever and wherever she performs. Betty E always puts out to the content of her spirit and to the pleasurable delight of her fans.

Whenever Betty E does what she do ... GOD gets the Glory!

Annetta Wilson, 63

NO APPROVAL COMMITTEE NEEDED

Annetta Wilson

> *"At age twenty, we worry about what others think of us. At age forty, we don't care what they think of us. At sixty, we discover they haven't been thinking of us at all."*
> *— Ann Landers*

If there's one quote that sums up the freedom of my sexy sixties, that's the one. The committee to approve of how I'm living my life doesn't exist. Coming to that realization near the beginning of my sixth decade was like being let out of prison. That revelation had me wishing I could travel back in time and give that piece of wisdom to my twenty-year-old self. Oh, the changes that would have sparked!

At the time of this writing, I'm sixty-two. Even looking at the number is weird, because I don't "feel" sixty-anything (presuming there's a feeling that goes with a certain age). The funny thing is, I don't get why some people freak out when they find out my age. Yes, I am thankful that "Black don't crack," and have been told that I look younger than my age (I certainly accept the compliment). What I find most amusing is what happens next; instead of continuing the conversation as before, there's a slight shift in their behavior. It's as if, now that they know how old I am, new rules of engagement have suddenly come into play. At that point, I chuckle to myself and hope they get some help for that.

Ageism is a thing. And I believe it's societal. In the West, we worship youth. In certain Eastern and African cultures, the elders are respected, even revered, and appreciated for their wisdom and beauty. I believe we have it backward in this country, and that is a missed opportunity for all age groups. That's why being a part of a project that celebrates women in their sixties is so exciting to me. It's one example that the tide is turning, realizing that with each birthday, a woman becomes more intriguing. Especially if she grows from the lessons and experiences time brings.

Getting to the place where my opinion of, and comfort with, myself outweighed other people's opinions, was not an easy road. On certain days, it can still be a thorn in my side. And, it's a reminder that I'm still a work in progress. However, before I arrived at the decision that loving and embracing who I am was more important than what people thought, I was an approval junkie — a people pleaser. In some cases, I was a chameleon that morphed into whoever I thought I needed to be in order to be liked. I spent a lot of my younger years in that exercise in futility. Part of it was the era in which I grew up: Segregation in the South in the 1960s and 1970s. I'm not going into a history lesson here (you should already know the impact of segregation. Don't wait for Black History Month to become enlightened). Being in my sexy sixties also allows me to keep it real. LOL

The philosopher Soren Kierkegaard once said, *"Life can only be understood backwards; but it must be lived forwards."* It's only in looking back that I realize the impact that time period had on my psyche. Imagine growing up in an environment when everything around you told you that you were not wanted, equal, or seen. My young mind believed that was true. That was a mistaken belief that would only be corrected with time.

It was the grace of God that I had parents who made home a safe haven. And, it was because I grew up in a church where the youth were encouraged to be leaders. My spiritual life grounds me to this day. Growing up in a segregated environment in Panama City, Florida, took its toll. Insecurity was the by-product. I tried to excel to be liked (mistake number one). I tried to fit in, even when it felt wrong (mistake number two). I believed people who said I wasn't good enough (the biggest mistake of them all!). Because of the crippling need to be liked and to fit in, I didn't allow myself to consider that being different, smart, and standing out were things to be celebrated, not run away from. At one point, I even tried to make bad grades, thinking that would help me fit in. Sadly, some of the people who tormented me most were people who looked like me. I was the chubby, glasses-wearing nerd — the perfect target for bullies. I thought I was destined to be a misfit, the weird kid. Later, I embraced it!

Looking back, I see how that spurred me on to excel. I wanted to prove them wrong. And it worked — in some areas of my life. School was one of them. I made good grades all the way through college. I think my motivation was more a fear of failure, rather than trying to achieve my personal best. Whatever motivates you, owns you. For me, that was getting approval from others. That is never a healthy place to be. The desire to fit in, and seek approval, haunted me for years.

I had disastrous relationships with people who I 'allowed' to make me feel as if I were lucky to be with them, and I said 'no' to opportunities that would have helped me grow personally and professionally because I was afraid of what people would think. I use the word 'allowed' intentionally. Because, no matter what anyone else said or did, the final decision about staying in a relationship with that person was mine. It's okay to feel your feelings. They're there, and you can't (or shouldn't) ignore them. Feelings are not good barometers to use in making big decisions. Feelings change. Remember to bring some truth, logic, and foresight to the table, too.

One of the biggest regrets that I based on feelings was not going on a trip to CBS headquarters in New York to meet then anchor, Dan Rather. I was a Broadcast Journalism major at Florida A & M University in Tallahassee. There was a controversy around that trip and a minor protest by some of the students. I don't even remember their names, or what the big deal was, yet I allowed what they thought to influence my decision not to go. There are times that I've wondered what that trip might have led to. I think about that decision with the knowledge I've gained over the years, that *every* decision I make in the present is building my future. There is no "neutral." It all counts.

I ended up meeting Dan Rather anyway, a few years later, when I was the evening news anchor for the CBS affiliate in Orlando. It was a little more satisfying at that point.

So, what does this trip down 'Memory Lane' have to do with my sexy sixties? Everything. If you don't look at the choices you've made in the past, and why you made them, you will likely find yourself in an endless cycle of "Groundhog Day." That's the movie starring Bill Murray when his character finds himself living the same day over and over again until he realizes that the madness will continue until he makes different choices. It's a very deep movie.

If there's anything I would say to a woman who has not reached her amazing sixth decade, it would be that the only person who needs to unconditionally approve of you, and the choices you make, is YOU. It is at once sobering and humbling, to finally understand that everyone else is busy doing them. No one is making their personal life decisions based on what you think. Why would you make choices about your life based on what THEY think?

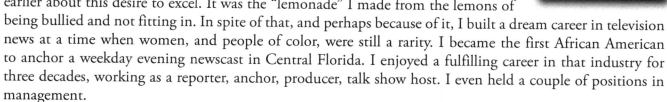

In full transparency, that didn't dawn on me until later in life, after doing a lot of introspective work. I am a huge fan of personal growth and development. I wrote earlier about this desire to excel. It was the "lemonade" I made from the lemons of being bullied and not fitting in. In spite of that, and perhaps because of it, I built a dream career in television news at a time when women, and people of color, were still a rarity. I became the first African American to anchor a weekday evening newscast in Central Florida. I enjoyed a fulfilling career in that industry for three decades, working as a reporter, anchor, producer, talk show host. I even held a couple of positions in management.

It's rather ironic that my current work, as a certified mastery coach and communication skills consultant, helps people embrace detractors, tell their insecurities, *"Thanks, but no thanks. I've got stuff to do!"* and go for it, in spite of the fear. I believe that because I understand what that feels like, I'm a more effective coach. Nothing is ever wasted.

Part of embracing my sexy sixties is about giving myself credit for what I've accomplished and overcome. You have to support and champion yourself in order to be in a healthy place. Still, that recognition has not come without a price. I've been married twice, neither of which I regret because I learned a lot about myself. I've made peace with the fact that I made the best choices I could make, given what I knew at the time. The tragedy would have been not learning anything and repeating the cycle.

Even when you know that something has run its course, that doesn't mean you won't hurt. It's part of being human. I believe pain is a reminder to pay closer attention to the choices you make next time. It eventually stops. Yes, I still believe in love. I have a wonderful man in my life who accepts all of me and doesn't try to change me. I'm a different woman at this stage in my life. And it's fantastic! Yes, my darlings, everything is better in your sexy sixties!

One of the things I embrace most about this time in my life is understanding that I cannot do it all myself. A support system of people who will call you on your stuff, while loving you forward, is not optional. It's mandatory. To think you don't need that 'checks and balance' system is an exercise in arrogance and narcissism. It's about making sure that in enjoying the freedom to be completely you, you don't damage other people in the process.

I am unabashedly unapologetic for the work I've done on my inner self. I've had a mentor for almost ten years. She has encouraged me to look at my patterns, dissect them, release the need for the ones that don't serve me, while giving myself compassion for being human. That work continues to help me grow. There is never a time when I feel like I know *enough*. What does that even mean? To me, it means that the moment I think I have it all figured out, game over! In my opinion, it's actually playing a dangerous game with God. I've seen too many of my plans go up in smoke or get completely turned around to feel that I always have things handled or figured out. Life doesn't operate that way. There's a quote that's been attributed to John

Lennon and Allen Saunders: *"Life is what happens to you while you're busy making other plans."* You'll never live long enough to know it all or make all the mistakes. Learn from the triumphs and experiences of others.

There's a humility that comes from entering your sixties. It places you at the interesting intersection of gratitude that you've made it this far, and the stark realization that there is more of your life behind you than ahead of you. It gets real at this point. At this stage of our lives, we have raised children and watched them launch into lives of their own; become caregivers to parents; lost people we loved; found ourselves at career crossroads or had health challenges we never saw coming.

It is still the best time of my life because I have learned so much. I have sons who still call me for advice. I'm a wonderful Mom, by their own admission. When I look back at raising my children, there's no better feeling than that. Getting to the point where I accepted myself as a wonderful mother was an exercise in asking myself questions as they were growing up: "Am I doing it right?", "Was I too strict here, not strict enough there?" On and on, ad nauseam. I learned to do the best I could in each moment, set rules, loved them, and allowed them to experience the consequences of their choices, whatever those choices happened to be. It was painful at times to not rescue them, but I knew that to do so would be sending the wrong message. It would only teach them to depend on other people to fix things for them. At this point in my life, I can look back and say that there's nothing I would have changed. Even my divorce from their father was one of the experiences that made me a more conscientious parent. At the time, my fear was that I was scarring them for life, and they'd never recover. I didn't, and they're amazing.

In truth, fear has been both a pain in the rear and a great motivator in my life. Not in the 'hide under the bed' sense, but in the sense that I don't want to have regrets. I don't want to look back someday and wonder what might have happened if only I had taken the chance, chosen a different path. . . blah, blah, blah.

As I look at what I just wrote, I almost laughed out loud. I understand, now, that wrestling with my fear took way more time than actually doing the thing that scared me. And the big, bad wolf that I was expecting to devour me, usually ended up being a cute little purse dog!

I have pushed myself to do things that scared me: A firewalk over thirty-feet of glowing red coals in my bare feet (without burning them); a flying trapeze; parasailing over the Caribbean Sea; rode on a snowmobile at seventy miles an hour (with an experienced rider); spent four hours walking through a forest with a group in complete silence (mind-blowing!); been inside a sweat lodge; rode on an elephant; and spoken to an audience of over three hundred people. And I'm STILL looking forward to my next adventure! Perhaps my biggest, never-ending adventure is the one within.

What I'm continuing to discover in this decade of my life is that my power is in my vulnerability. It sounds like an oxymoron, yet it makes sense. I've learned that when I am strong enough to show someone my flaws and moments of uncertainty, that's when I have a deeper connection with them. And now we're back full circle to the vulnerability of that little girl growing up in Panama City all of those years ago. It always comes back to where it began. That's where the healing is, that's where the ghosts are, that's the place where you first feel your sense of self. It's where you take your first faltering steps into adulthood and become curious about the bigger world. And, it never leaves you, even if you leave IT.

Looking back, I think that's why I never missed a high school reunion, except when I was about to deliver a baby. Those reunions became my litmus test for how much I had grown. With everything I'd accomplished, there was still a part of me that needed to prove something. There's something a bit magical about this stage of my life. The need to prove anything to anyone has been replaced by the need to become a better version of myself — for me and for those I love.

If I were to attend another class reunion, it would be for the sheer joy of connecting and reminiscing, laughing at our silly antics, and being grateful we made it this far. There's also something about making peace with your past. If you like where the journey has taken you (and I do), then why not make peace with it? It is what got you to this point. Every moment of joy, every tear, every person, and experience contributed to this amazing pot of gumbo that is my life. I've created fulfilling relationships, and I've let some relationships go. I would not have had the courage to do either of those without taking a hard look at myself.

Embracing my sexy sixties means there's still more to do. I'm happy that my family and friends have applauded the changes in my life over the years. I'm thankful they have been there through it all. The most important part is that 'I' applaud the changes, and the journey it took to get there.

Can't wait to see what the next decade brings! Look out!

Annetta Wilson is President of Annetta Wilson Media Training & Success Coaching (www.SpeakWithEase.com). She is a business strategist specializing in media training, presentation and communication skills coaching for executives, entrepreneurs and subject-matter experts.

Ms. Wilson was a performance coach for on-air journalists at CNN; coached for Walt Disney World's Ambassador Program and I.T. specialists; and conducted trainings for AAA, Tupperware Brands, Inc., the Orlando Magic, the University of Central Florida and Delta Dental, among others.

Annetta holds the distinction of being the first African-American to anchor a weekday evening newscast in Central Florida (CBS affiliate WKMG-TV). During her award-winning career in the broadcast industry, she held positions as a reporter, producer, talk show host and writer. Ms. Wilson held management positions in the broadcast industry as a community affairs director and marketing director.

She is a Certified Mastery Coach and Certified Trainer, and is the creator of *'You've Got Less Than 15 Seconds. Impress Me!'* (elevator speech system). She is known for her high-energy, highly interactive workshops and trainings.

Ms. Wilson was honored by the Orlando Business Journal as one of Central Florida's 'Women Who Mean Business'. She has been a guest editorial writer for the Orlando Sentinel newspaper.

She serves on the Board of Directors for Heart of Florida United Way, Give Kids the World, and the Board of Visitors for the School of Journalism and Graphic Communication at her alma mater, Florida A&M University.

Annetta was national emcee for the Office Depot Success Strategies Conference for Businesswomen in six major U.S. cities. She is one of 8 coaches featured in the book, *'Coaching for Success'* (Insight Publishing) and is member of the International Association of Coaching. She is the author of the upcoming book, *'Say Less. Talk More'* (Tips to Communicate for Power and Influence).

Miriam D. Martin, MD. 62

PHYSICIAN, HEAL THYSELF

Miriam D. Martin, MD

I sat there and wondered to myself, *what am I doing here?* And then I thought, *doctors' waiting rooms need to have an interior designer.* Most waiting rooms that I had experienced at that time were not so aesthetically pleasing. Mental note to myself: *This is something to suggest to some of my fellow doctors.* The receptionist just told me that the doctor would be with me in a few minutes. There were several patients in front of me. I told myself to relax. I closed my eyes and took a deep breath. Again, how did I get here? My mind started to wander. It was not like I had not been here before. That time, I had been that skeptical patient that thinks she knows more than the doctor. After all, I am a doctor and had been practicing medicine for years. I was reminded of the words, "Physician, Heal Thyself." The fact that many people do not know the actual meaning of this phrase, including many physicians, amuses me.

Physician, Heal Thyself could be extrapolated to mean that before you venture out into the world to heal others, you should probably heal yourself first. In other words, before a physician could adequately cure the diseases that others are experiencing, they must first cure their own. Physicians are fiercely hard-working, intelligent, resilient, and self-sufficient. That's how we became doctors. Yet, these same characteristics that got us into medical school are also the very reason that we don't ask for the help that we may need. There is an expectation that physicians should be able to fix their own problems. In other words, because of their personalities and a certain level of expectations, doctors may have a hard time seeking help. In truth, "Physician, Heal Thyself" can be an inappropriate ideology. Like anyone else, physicians deal with burnout, depression, and stress, and, therefore, may require healing from someone other than themselves.

I began to shift in my seat and reflected again as to why I was here waiting to see the doctor. Yes, I was Miriam D. Martin, MD, but like other physicians, I was also human. My mind filtered back to my life in Detroit. I smiled at the memory that I had come from a musical background, playing multiple instruments since the fourth grade. Upon entering Northwestern High School in Detroit, Michigan, I met my Biology teacher, Mrs. Clay. She detected something in me that I had never even remotely considered.

She planted the seed of medicine as a career. I always excelled in Math and Science and took all of the college academic preparatory courses available. But music was in my spirit and my soul. My high school was a magnet school for fine arts. We were well known in the area for being a musical powerhouse in both classical and jazz genres. We amazed the judges at the Band and Orchestra festivals with our top scores in classical music, as we were an all-Black Band and Orchestra from the inner city of Detroit. My instruments du jour were clarinet and violin. I spent a great deal of time playing in my school band and orchestra, as well as in the Detroit Youth Symphony. The rest of the time, my head was buried in Chemistry, Biology, Physics, and Mathematics books. Even today, if someone were to ask me "Why Medicine?" I smile and think about Mrs. Clay. I wonder if she realized what a huge part she played in my success.

I stand to stretch and walk to get a cup of water. I gaze outside and I am reminded of the day that I came to Washington, D.C.

As an exceptionally gifted student in Detroit, my grades allowed me to attend most any college that I chose. I was a Detroiter, and anyone claiming to be from Detroit knew what that meant. There was a pride in being black in Detroit during the 1970s. Detroit was the most populous city in Michigan, with a population of approximately 1.8 million people, of which eighty percent were black. We had the highest per capita income in the United States. In 1976, when I graduated from high school, Coleman Young was the Mayor. He was the city's first African American Mayor and was widely popular. Black success was part of my DNA as a Detroiter. So, it was no accident that I chose to attend Howard University – the "Black Mecca."

Howard University is considered the most prestigious Historically Black College or University (HBCU) in the United States. Their College of Medicine is internationally regarded for its illustrious legacy of training students to become competent and compassionate physicians. They provide health care in medically underserved communities at home and abroad. The College is a national leader in studying health disparities among people of color and is one of America's top institutions for training women physicians. Howard rested on a hilltop just two miles from the U.S. Capitol; far enough to say that I went away to college, but close enough to be near home if necessary. In every sense of the word, life was good — or at least it appeared to be.

My life story could have really been entitled, "The Tale of Two Doctors." One doctor successfully acquired two degrees from Howard – Bachelor of Science in Chemistry and Doctor of Medicine. This doctor also completed an Emergency Medicine Residency at Howard University Hospital, and subsequently, became an Associate Professor at the institution. Doctor number one was an attending physician at various hospitals in D.C., Maryland, and Virginia and eventually opened her own medical practice – the M.D. Medical and Wellness Center — which offered a variety of services, including family medicine, weight loss, and aesthetics to name a few. Yes, this doctor had it going on! Then there was the other doctor who was now sitting, not so patiently, awaiting her moment with the medical professional. By virtue of being there, the other doctor had to admit somehow; she could not heal "thyself."

Life was a little overwhelming, although, on the outside, one would never know. She had been masking things so well—.until now.

I rose from my seat to inquire from the receptionist as to how much longer it would be until I was seen. Upon checking, she informed me that there were now only two people ahead of me. She apologized again for the delay. I smiled at her and told her that it was okay. It was not her fault, so there was no way to take it out on her. I realized that I needed some air. I let her know that I was going to step outside for a moment. She smiled as if she understood. She looked like she probably wanted a break also. I stepped outside and surveyed the scenery. It was a beautiful, warm spring day. This was one of my favorite seasons in the DMV.

I loved Spring and Fall. But most of all, I loved the cherry blossoms. The cherry blossom trees are, without a doubt, the stars of springtime in Washington, D.C. During my first Spring in the area, as a

Howard student, I was told that during the National Cherry Blossom Festival, the most popular place to visit the cherry blossom trees was at the Tidal Basin. I discovered that the majority of blossoms are located near the Tidal Basin and along the shoreline of East Potomac Park, extending to Hains Point. I smile to myself as I remember all of the photos that I had taken each year as I succumbed to my favorite pastime. The smile began to fade as I massaged my temples and tried to shift my thoughts. That was becoming more difficult each day, hence, why I was even here. Where had the tale gone wrong?

What was wrong was my inability to comprehend at that time, that physicians are human, too. In my mind, I was a superhero with a stethoscope. I did not want to admit that I had experienced challenging marital and professional situations. How could I? To the outside world, the fairy tale was real. For me, I was living by the Serenity Prayer:

> *God, grant me the serenity to accept the things I cannot change;*
> *Courage to change the things I can,*
> *And the wisdom to know the difference.*

I pushed to change the things that I could, and that was taking care of my children by providing for them and shielding them from anything that was not part of the fairy tale. I pushed the envelope, which resulted in a work-life imbalance. The demands of working two, and sometimes, three jobs were, at times, overwhelming. It did not matter. No one could see a chink in my armor. I was so busy taking care of everyone else, that I somehow failed to take care of myself. The house, the cars, private schooling, and all of the expensive gadgets does not make one happy. My grandmother used to tell me that money could not buy you happiness. I thought at the time; she just doesn't know where to shop. I now realize what she meant. I also soon realized that I never paid attention to the last part of the serenity prayer, the wisdom to know the difference. How can I be this smart in some areas of my life and so inadequate when it came to taking care of me?

Something was wrong. I was just feeling off. Nothing I could really put my finger on; it was just off. But how do I fix it? I called my doctor to make an appointment.

I now know what it feels like when my patients come to me and say, '*I am not sure, but something is wrong.*' I told her that things just didn't feel right. She insisted that I come in so that she could take a look at me for herself. She needed to ascertain whether I was still combing my hair, ironing my clothes, putting on makeup, and the like. Upon arriving at her office, I was asked by her medical assistant the reason for my visit. I told her I was feeling depressed. Her assistant, whom I have never seen and who knew nothing about me, replied, "There is nothing wrong with you; you just need Jesus." I remember feeling offended, and as if she was belittling my complaint and how it was affecting me. How dare she respond to me in that manner. However, it would not be long before I realized that she was right!

My doctor recognized the signs of burnout and wrote me a referral. That referral led me to this very same waiting room. Initially, like most physicians, I was in denial. Her diagnosis was a common one – major depression. Many doctors suffer from it, and many were in denial, just like me. They refuse to change or heed the advice necessary to heal themselves. She prescribed medication and suggested considering therapy. I thanked her politely at that time. Was she crazy? She did not know me like that. I was Dr. Miriam D. Martin, and I was not taking the medications that she prescribed. Admittedly, I am not that bad. She had only seen me once. All I needed was some talk therapy. Anti-depressants are only for those individuals who had it really bad – surely, that was not me.

However, I was not getting any better. I required more than a Band-Aid – I needed some serious intervention. I pulled out my DSM (Diagnostic and Statistical Manual of Mental Disorders) and began reviewing the signs and symptoms of depression. I fit almost all of the diagnostic criteria:

- Depressed mood most of the day
- Diminished interest or pleasure in most or all activities
- Change in appetite
- Fatigue and loss of energy
- Feelings of worthlessness or inappropriate guilt
- Diminished ability to concentrate

It appeared the only symptom I did not have was thoughts of committing suicide. However, for the first time in my life, I could understand what could drive someone to want to end it all. In fact, I have medical school classmates who are not here today due to their decision to commit suicide. This little trip through my DSM made it crystal clear to me that I, indeed, had it bad. Had it not been for my children, maybe I would have decided just to give up. However, they were the driving force that kept me going through it all.

I journeyed back to the waiting room. This was my second visit, and I must admit, I am a much more compliant patient this time. I am not only willing to take her advice, but also the medication. Most physicians, like myself, who take these steps are on the road to finding the true meaning of the phrase "Physician, Heal Thyself" — and the true meaning is that physicians *cannot* completely heal themselves. Sometimes, we need help just like anyone else. Just then, they called my name, "Dr. Miriam Martin, the doctor, will see you now."

That day seems like a million years ago, and it also feels just like yesterday. This newfound freedom has allowed me to reshape both my work life and my personal life. However, there was a part of the prescription that my doctor could not fill. It turns out that annoying medical assistant was right. I did need Jesus. There are certain aspects where your spiritual life helps in the recovery of the depression process. A religious framework and a belief in God can help us maintain hope, even when the road is long. I was blessed to find a church home that was committed to not just preaching, but also teaching the Word of God and making it applicable to my life. This was a new and much-needed concept for me. Although I had grown up in church, the church had not grown up in me. I began to thirst for the Word and enrolled and graduated from the Christian College at the church. It was there that it was revealed to me the spiritual aspect of healing and how to incorporate that into my practice. I eventually became part of the leadership of the church. I served as an Armor Bearer to my pastor and as a member of the Deacon Board.

Slowly, but surely, that cloud of depression dissipated to be replaced by a feeling of peace and tranquility. Through my faith in Christ, I was able to hold steadfast to the belief that positive change can occur and that it is not just wishful thinking. The reality is that you know that you can never give up. You can do everything in your power to be free of depression, but sometimes, in my case, you have to practice acceptance and realize that you can't win the fight alone. By engaging in spiritual practices, prayer, attending church service, or simply spending time with nature amid the cherry blossoms, you can experience a positive change in attitude and behaviors that will help you fight depression. When you view your life as having a spiritual path, problems are not an obstacle, but instead, opportunities for growth and learning. You end up knowing that you are right where you need to be at any given moment.

I now realized that I did not have to be perfect. In reality, I did not need to change so much, as I needed to clear away some confusion so that my true self could shine through. This new peace also let me know that I did not always have to be on the go. I found in my spirituality a quiet part of myself. Sometimes, the best thing to do is to accept where you are and simply do nothing.

I spend my sixties with a servitude attitude. I am serving my community as a proud member of Alpha Kappa Alpha Sorority, Incorporated, the first Black female, Greek organization. As Co-Chairman of the Health Committee, I have been responsible for leading my chapter in raising awareness of health issues affecting African American women. Some of these events have included breast cancer and mental health symposiums, mobile mammogram screening, CPR instruction and certification, various exercise activities, and recognizing the caregivers in our organization. I had the honor and distinction of leading Team IGO AKA (Iota Gamma Omega Chapter) as we became the number one fundraiser for two consecutive years at the annual National Alliance of Mental Illness' Maryland NAMIWalk. I enjoy mentoring young women, and I am a preceptor for medical assistants and nurse practitioners. I am also very involved and committed to my church, the City of Praise Family Ministries. I serve as part of the Leadership Team and as the head of the Singles' Ministry. I jokingly refer to myself as a "professional single". Truthfully, I have not given up on the institution of marriage. I am just not rushing it, as I am in a good place right now, just being with me. Should marriage become a reality in my life, I am sure I will share that journey as well. Three children, one daughter-in-love, and three grandchildren later, I have finally learned the true meaning of joy.

As the late and great Apostle Betty P. Peebles taught me, "Joy is an inward stability that God, through Jesus Christ, fortified by the Holy Spirit, on my behalf, has already worked it out!" This simply means that I can be happy, despite the situation and despite what it may look like. It is not in my hands – it is in God's!

At this writing, I am serving on the frontline in the capacity of an emergency medicine physician and family practitioner during the 2020 COVID-19 pandemic. I disseminate information via live updates on social media to provide factual information and updates on this horrific illness, which is disproportionately affecting black and brown communities. This is a very stressful time for America and the world at large. It is a time of great economic, physical, and psychological turmoil. In addition, it has caused a separation from myself and my family as we self-isolate in different parts of the country. One of the most favorite things to do – visit my family – has been stripped away due to the Coronavirus Pandemic. On the bright side, I am "virtually" able to see and speak to them every day via numerous social medial platforms.

Because of my faith, I am able to endure this season of strife without fear or experiencing the depression I once knew in the past. This seasoned lady is able to wake up in the morning with a smile on her face and joy in her heart. I am more keenly aware in my sixties that life is not so much about me, as it is about others. This physician has learned to **heal** herself so that she may continue with her mission of healing others.

*M*riam D. Martin, MD. is a seasoned emergency medicine and family practice specialist with a passion for promoting total health and wellness.

A native of Detroit, Michigan, Dr. Martin has earned both her Bachelor of Science Degree in Chemistry and her Medical Degree from Howard University. She received her training in Emergency Medicine at Howard University Hospital.

Dr. Martin is currently the medical director of MD Medical and Wellness Center in Prince George's County, MD. She also practices emergency medicine in the District of Columbia, Maryland, and Virginia.

Dr. Martin hosts The Medical Message – a weekly social media broadcast focusing on the spiritual and physical well-being of her audience.

She is a member of Alpha Kappa Alpha Sorority, Inc. and serves on the Executive Committee of her local chapter as well as having served as Chairman of their Health Concerns Committee. In this role she has organized numerous health events, including blood drives, mental health seminars, and breast cancer screenings. She and her team were responsible for raising the most money in the state of Maryland for two consecutive years at the NAMIWalks Maryland for mental illness.

Dr. Martin is active in her church, the City of Praise Family Ministries, and is a member of their Leadership Team. She is the mother of three and the grandmother of three more. In her spare time she enjoys traveling, exercising, and spending time with family and friends.

Dr. Martin is fully committed to the health and wellness of our communities and serving in any capacity which promotes spiritual and physical well-being.

Rev. Dr. D. Amina B. Butts, 65

WONDERFUL AND AMAZING!

Rev. Dr. D. Amina B. Butts

> *"… you made me in an amazing and wonderful way."*
> *-Psalm 139:14 (NCV)*

What has sixty-five years of living taught me?

What message to the world can I give that the Universe has chosen to teach me? What do I know to be true? What is it that I know — that I know that I know? What I know to be true is that life has taught me what I've needed to learn, and those lessons have been invaluable.

As a spiritual being having a human experience, I've seen the hand of God working in my life from my earliest existence. At just four years old, I felt the profound presence of God, and then again at age twenty-eight, thirty, and throughout my life. But I've also felt God's absence, I've felt pain, and I've felt despair. This has caused me to appreciate the light and the dark, the ups and the downs, the sweet and the sour . . . you know, those hallelujah good times! As well as those times when you find yourself bone-tired and soul-weary.

THE CHILDHOOD YEARS

I was a very quiet child. I was actually painfully shy. Because I was so shy, I often just wanted to hide. I could be in a room, and you wouldn't even know that I was there. But despite my shyness, there was always something in me that wanted to express itself.

When I was in the sixth grade, I remember running for class president. And guess what? I won!

I was often afraid, but I pushed through those feelings.

Like many teenagers, I couldn't seem to find my place. I had friends, but I still didn't feel like I belonged. I hung around with the "bad" kids, and I did some "bad" things, too.

But ever since I was a child, my real friends were books. In high school, I had a Black History teacher named Mr. Thomas. He whetted my appetite for learning more about my culture. This led to my choosing African Studies as a major in college, before later switching to Criminology. I was asked, "What are you going to do with a degree in African Studies?" I didn't have an answer, so I changed course. I decided that I really wanted to go to law school.

MY TRYING IT OUT TWENTIES

My twenties went by in a blur; they were punctuated by work and an active social life. My first job after college was at the Department of Health, Education and Welfare (DHEW), where I was employed as a program analyst in the Medicaid Program.

Later, I worked in a program for women in non-traditional jobs. My responsibility was to monitor programs throughout the country in Boston, New Orleans, Providence, RI, and Oakland, CA; I enjoyed the traveling.

One day, I was having lunch in the park, as many government workers did. Sitting there, I met a very handsome young man who decided he wanted to talk to me. We struck up a conversation, and he asked me for my number. He was a graduate of Howard University, and he was from St. Thomas, Virgin Islands. He also was about to be commissioned as an Army Officer. The young man and I began to date, and as time went on, we decided to get married. After our wedding and honeymoon, my husband, who was now a commissioned officer, was assigned to Ft. Sill, Oklahoma. So, I moved way across the country to Oklahoma with a man from the Virgin Islands, an Army Officer, who became my first husband. However, the marriage was filled with drama, and we divorced not long after moving to Oklahoma.

Because I had a job that I loved, I stayed in Oklahoma with no family, but new friends. I bought a house and settled as best as I could into a community that was far different from the East Coast. While I was divorced, I didn't stay unmarried for long. I remarried, this time to a man seven years my junior, an enlisted Army Chaplain Assistant. When I married him, I had on all black — not a good sign.

My job as a substance abuse coordinator and counselor was demanding. Daily, I had to give substance abuse prevention talks to hundreds of service members, as well as facilitate recovery groups during the week and even on Saturdays. As I looked out into the audience at these young soldiers, I saw the most lonely and forlorn faces I had ever seen. I began to talk to them about the love of God in Jesus Christ. This was not on the script, but it was in my heart to evangelize and save the lost. I had started preaching on the job!

But what happened next changed my life forever. My husband asked me to speak on Father's Day at the church that he pastored. I had been feeling the hand of God on my life, but I had kept it to myself.

When I spoke on Father's Day, my young husband told his congregation, "I prayed for help. I didn't know that it was here all the time."

THRILLING THIRTIES?

When I was thirty, I had major surgery, a hysterectomy. It was not a good experience; not only was it filled with a painful recovery, but for years after the surgery, my emotions were often all over the place. I began to suffer from deep, dark, depressive episodes. God often felt absent and even cruel. God was no longer the kind and benevolent being that I expected Him to be. Where was God in my storm? How could I go on during these times of despair? I began to feel "stuck," and my traditional religious practices weren't working. I began to question everything. I suffered intensely, and each day was filled with grief and sorrow. I cried for help, but there was no relief. I had what St. John of the Cross calls "The Dark Night of the Soul."

I quit my job, lost my house, and moved back home to the DMV (the District of Columbia, Maryland, and Virginia) with my husband. We moved in with my parents. I moved through the depression by throwing myself into the ministry. At age thirty-three, I entered seminary, and then as I was about to get settled into a life of academia and ministry, my husband says he wants a divorce. How could this be happening a second time? My husband was a high school graduate, and his wife was college-educated and about to enter her second year as a seminary student. It was way too much for his male ego. My mother came over to our apartment, and I told her what had happened. Her response surprised me, for she said, "Maybe now you can do what God has called you to do."

I graduated from seminary at thirty-six; I was the second youngest person in my class. My father in the ministry expected a lot of me. One day, he looked at me and spoke these words into my life: "You're going to go far."

FABULOUS FORTIES!

My forties became a time of self-discovery and a continuing battle with depression. I was selected to become the first woman chaplain at the Maryland Correctional Institution for Women (MCIW). On the way to the interview, my car broke down. I was stranded until someone stopped to help, and miraculously, they were able to get the car started. I made it to the interview, but I was late. I was one of forty applicants, but I got the job! God's hand was on my life.

Working with incarcerated women was one of the most challenging and exhilarating times of my life. Although most were victims of their circumstances, such as poverty, they had spunk, they had grace, and they had personal power. Sometimes I would meet women who were incarcerated together with their sisters, their cousins, and even their mothers. I met pregnant women and women living with HIV, all living in four squares — getting three meals and a cot.

Emotions run raw in prison, and everything is out in the open. Your deep-seated feelings come to the surface. I began to identify with the women I ministered to; this could be me, but for the grace of God. Have you ever been so angry that you wanted to kill the person next to you?

Sometimes, that's exactly what had happened; a fit of rage, self-defense, all understandable and reflexive responses to emotional abuse.

Sexuality is open for display in prison. Young women, many my age or younger, were residents of MCIW. I began to get in touch with an aspect of my sexuality that I had never tapped into. I experienced strong physical attractions to women. What was happening? Luckily for me, I was led to professionals that helped to reassure me that there was nothing wrong with me. But it took years of therapy, biblical scholarship, personal work, and relationships to come to terms with my budding sexuality. Eventually, and over time, I began to realize that God had given me an expanded capacity to love. I could love a man, and I could love a woman, too. I learned that I am wonderful and amazing!

The discovery of the importance of self-love continued to be the hallmark of my journey to complete and total wholeness. Loving my black self, my natural black self, meant that harsh chemicals would no longer touch my head. Just before heading to my first trip to the Motherland, to Senegal and the Gambia, I locked my hair. Throughout my forties and my fifties, I wore my hair locked, growing it all the way down to my waist.

On February 12, 2005, at 5 p.m., at the Spirit House in Washington, D.C., a ministry led by an incredible activist, Ruby Nell Sales, I changed my name. "Lord, I know I been changed! The angels in heaven done signed my name!" On this day, on my fiftieth birthday, I took on a new name, Amina Binta. What's in a name? In antiquity, it was believed that the character or identity of a person was expressed in a name. The name of a person represented the innermost self or identity of a person. The naming of a child was important, and when a person went through a transforming experience, he or she was given a new name.

If one wanted to know someone personally, it was necessary to know that person's name (Understanding the Old Testament, Bernhard W. Anderson).

I went through a transforming experience at age fifty. It was then that I received the Doctor of Ministry degree (DMin) from the Wesley Theological Seminary in Washington, D.C. The title of my dissertation was "Why We Can't Wait: The Quest for Intentional Inclusion in a Black Baptist Church." It is a study of how the intentional inclusion of women, youth, the differently-abled, those of disparate economic backgrounds, varied religious practices, and same-gender-loving persons can lead to a church that fully embraces the mandate of the church of Jesus Christ. It was a groundbreaking study that helped prepare the congregation for the installation of the first female pastor at Covenant Baptist Church, the Rev. Dr. Christine Y. Wiley and the marriage of the first openly gay couple at a Black Baptist Church in the District of Columbia.

The work was transforming; it revitalized the congregation, as was I, in the process. It was time to take on a new name.

MY NEW NAME

This new name, Amina Binta, came to me in the night. What I heard was that I would begin to use this name as I took on my identity as a writer. I knew very little about the name when it came to me. What I have since learned is that Amina (also Aminatu, and I go by Aminata, too) was a Hausa warrior queen. She ruled in the mid-sixteenth century. Amina distinguished herself and gained notoriety for her military skills. She is celebrated in traditional Hausa praise songs as "Amina, daughter of Nikatau, a woman as capable as a man." (Wikipedia). Amina is a common West African name, as common as the name Mary. Amina means honest, trustworthy, and truthful. It is a lot to live up to, but it suits me perfectly. If you do not want to know the truth, then do not ask me.

Binta is a name that means 'African Queen; she loves her friends and family, and she will fight for anything that bothers her, including her family and friends. She isn't afraid of anyone…' (Urban Dictionary). And yes, I am a warrior, and I'm not afraid of anyone. Binta also means daughter of, or with God. That gives me assurance and comfort.

The ceremony was performed by Bishop Kwabena Rainey Cheeks, an Akan priest, and the Rev. Queen Mutima Imani, a Native American medicine woman, who flew in from California to do the ceremony. In attendance were members of my immediate family, as well as my extended family of Liberian cousins, and a host of special friends were there, too. The energy was palpable; I can still hear those very drum beats as African dancers, Nana Malaya, and others twisted and jumped and invoked the presence of the Ancestors.

In 2013, I founded the Believe Center for Change.

The Believe Center for Change is a faith-based organization that provides educational and wellness services to children and their families. In 2014, the Believe Center for Change traveled to Liberia, West Africa. Finally, I found myself in this ancestral place that I had heard about all of my life. I went there to form a partnership with a local HIV provider, to spend three nights preaching at a local church full of sex workers, to visit two local schools, and to spend time with my cousin, Dolly.

Today, the Believe Center for Change continues to provide educational services to both the McDaniel Faith Academy and the Tower of Faith Ministries in Paynesville, Liberia. It has been a blessing to support the school that was named after the father of my childhood friend, Dr. L. Akilah Karima McDaniel, who died in 2019. Pastor Martin V. Payne, Sr. and I have formed a close bond.

He is like a brother to me, and his wife is like a sister.

The wellness piece of the center is critical to my own well-being. I am a Master Reiki Teacher and Practitioner, a yoga, qigong, and Tai Chi enthusiast, and a Certified Optimal Life Breathologist.

Reiki has saved my life. I had debilitating pain that was healed through the modality of Reiki. The more I take the time to simply just breathe, the more amazing and wonderful that I am!

MY SEXY SIXTIES

For my sixtieth birthday, I went on a cruise to the Bahamas with a man that I had fallen in love with. We had been dating for three years, and I wanted to get married. He clearly indicated that wasn't what he wanted, but I ignored both what he said and what he did or didn't do. However, the unexpected gift of this relationship was that because he couldn't love me, I learned to love myself. I learned to tell myself that I look good. I learned to look myself in the mirror and tell myself that I am beautiful. I am beautiful whether my hair is to my waist, as it was when I was in my fifties, or if I am without hair, as I have been throughout my sexy sixties. For, if I waited to hear it from him, I was going to have to wait a really long time.

At sixty-five, I am still single, but I am expecting love to happen *for* me and *to* me. I love myself enough not to settle; I won't allow anyone to mistreat the God within me! Today, I know that life is to be lived fully until your last breath. I know that the world really is your oyster, but you've got to *get up* and *harvest* your oysters.

What I have learned, as I embrace my sexy sixties, is that my spirituality and my sexuality are both powerful forces of nature.

My spirituality means that I love myself first. Loving myself means that I practice self-care. It means that not only do I have a Reiki practice, but I do Reiki on myself, too. It means getting massages, practicing yoga, playing tennis, hula hooping, taking singing lessons, going for long walks in nature, having my nails done, and always looking my best.

And what about my sexuality? What have I learned as I embrace my sexy sixties? Well, sex has been the biggest surprise of all — at sixty-five, I have a healthy sex life, and as I get older, the sexier I feel! God created sex, and sex is good! Sex is good for you, too.

Not only that, but at sixty-five, I am also healthy and whole. At sixty-five . . . *I am wonderful and amazing!*

A life-long learner, the Rev. Dr. D. Amina B. Butts earned the Doctor of Ministry (DMin) degree from the Wesley Theological Seminary, where she was the only black woman to earn that degree in 2005. She received her Master of Divinity (MDiv) degree from the Howard University School of Divinity, and was the recipient of the Ford Foundation Grant for Outstanding Women in Ministry. She received a Master of Arts in Teaching (MAT) degree from Trinity Washington University and a Bachelor of Arts (BA) degree in Criminology from the University of Maryland, College Park. Currently, Dr. Butts is in pursuit of the Juris Doctorate degree. Dr. Butts was certified as a special educator and elementary teacher in both Washington, D.C. and Maryland. For over thirty years she has pursued her passion for developing young learners.

Dr. Butts has had a storied career as an administrator. She directed the Women's Empowerment Program at the Alexandria Detention Center and the Community Continuum Program at the Institute for Behavior Change and Research (IBCR), an HIV program for women living with mental illness, substance abuse and HIV.

Rev. Dr. Butts has also had a thirty-year career as a pastor, serving in churches and institutions throughout Maryland, the District of Columbia and Oklahoma. Rev. Butts served as an Army Chaplain, a full-time prison chaplain at the Maryland Correctional Institution for Women, and as the oncology chaplain at the Washington Hospital Center and the Children's National Medical Center.

Dr. Butts is a Master Reiki Teacher and Practitioner, a yoga, Tai Chi and Qigong enthusiast, an Optimal Life Breathologist, and a lover of the arts. She is the Founder of the Believe Center for Change, a faith-based non-profit.

Born in Washington, D.C., Dr. Amina currently resides in Takoma Park, MD, but her ancestral home is in Liberia, West Africa.

Debbie Morris, 60

THE VILLAGE IN MY LIFE THAT GROUNDED ME

Debbie Morris

Embracing my sixties means accepting the person that I am, appreciating the road I took to get here, and welcoming the adventure ahead of me. There was a time when sixty seemed old to me, but now, I embrace it. I don't feel old. In fact, inside me still lives that adventurous, tireless dynamo, not ever content with standing still. That part of me hasn't changed since I was a child. It's part of my DNA.

FAMILY FUNDAMENTALS

I was a go-getter for as long as I can remember. I was Joanne Welcher-Morris's oldest child and my father's middle daughter. I was a big sister and an aunt by the time I was three years old. That made me a nurturer and protector for most of my life. I come from a family of strong women, who perhaps, developed their fortitude not by choice, but by circumstance and necessity. My mother was a single parent, yet she did not raise us alone; I grew up with my grandparents, so someone was always home for us. We weren't upper middle class by any means, but we had everything we needed, and probably lived much more comfortably than many of the other kids in the neighborhood. As I look back now, I'm amazed at all we had as children. We went to private school, we always had enough food to eat and clothes to wear, and we were never short on love.

At the risk of sugar-coating my childhood, I know it couldn't have been easy for my Mom. My parents were divorced when I was very small. It couldn't have been easy to find herself raising two children without their father. Still, I can honestly say, not once did my mother ever say anything negative about our father. She accepted the circumstances, and I'm sure having her parents, my grandparents, Fred and Katie Welcher, to help raise us, made life a lot less stressful for her. My grandmother, Katie, was a strict disciplinarian, yet loving.

I'm sure being surrounded by single women, many of whom were raising daughters on their own, had a significant influence on me. From my Mom's perspective, we had to be self-sufficient and self-reliant. I watched her work, take college classes, and carve out a life of adventure and purpose. It's incredible, but never do I ever recall her complaining about life. Her dream was her two daughters. To this day, my sister, Denise, and I make sure she has everything possible that we can give. We don't have to say it, and she doesn't have to ask.

Her advice for us has always been to set goals and stay on the path to accomplish them. Sometimes there are detours you have to work around. Grow from them and keep moving. Her path for my sister and me was drawn early on. Like any good Mom, she wanted more for us than she could even imagine for herself. I think that what kept my sister and me out of trouble was the fear of ever disappointing our Mom or causing her any pain. Doing something to hurt ourselves would be the ultimate pain for her. She didn't have to tell us this. We just knew how much we meant to her.

My Mom is a beautiful ninety-one-year-old woman. I've come to appreciate her more and more each day. We can now talk about our shared life experiences, especially now that I've reached my sixties. What I know now that I didn't know about my Mom before is that our passions, our drive, our love of life don't diminish with age. There are always new reasons to want to live our life to the fullest. She gives me inspiration and a reason to believe the best is yet to come.

We are all a product of our childhood and how we were raised. And since my childhood was divided between two families, my Mom's and my Dad's, there were a number of influences, and again, most of them were strong women. They were the glue that kept this blended family together — that included me and my father's children: Barbara, Gloria, Denise, Buddy, and Katrina. My two older half-sisters, Barbara and Gloria, and their Mom looked after me. Because they were determined to maintain that bond, all of my father's children remain close to this day. All of my father's daughters and their daughters, Janina and Angela, share a common characteristic. Independence, for us, didn't mean wanting to be alone. It was more about not allowing ourselves to ever be lonely, whether we had partners or not. Loneliness was more a state of mind than a state of being. I can't stress enough how important family has been to me and how it's shaped my life. My aunts were like surrogate mothers, and my cousin, Jean, was more like the older sister, watching us grow and enjoying our every accomplishment as if they were her own.

While I was raised to be independent, my Mom and all of the other women in my life, more than likely had similar hopes and dreams for the girls they were raising. It may not have been explicitly expressed, but I do believe they hoped that we would find men who would cherish us and be wonderful fathers to our children.

THE NORTH CAROLINA CHAPTER

If life was a fairy tale book, I thought this was the chapter for me. By the age of twenty-one, I believed I had met the man of my dreams, a young dental student, and Army Captain. It was a whirlwind romance. The next thing I knew, I was pregnant and off to North Carolina, leaving behind my family and friends, and everything that was familiar and safe. Amazingly, even after giving birth and transferring to a different university, I was still able to graduate from college in four years. Finishing college was a promise I made to my Mom, so I was not going to let her down. Attending graduate school while raising two children was yet another accomplishment.

This new phase in my life, being a wife and mother, turned out to be a significant turning point in my life. I had embraced this part of my life. I enjoyed sharing a home and the responsibility of raising our children with my husband. I was going to live happily ever after. It turns out, the fairy tale in my head proved to be more fantasy than reality.

By the time I was twenty-eight, I was already the mother of a daughter, pregnant with my son, and about to learn my life was a mirage. I was about to become a statistic. My marriage became the victim of my husband's infidelity. Notice, I didn't say I was the victim. I was determined not to be. I was devastated for my daughter and my unborn son, but I didn't want them to be victims either. My children, Toya and Billy, needed a strong, self-sufficient, and self-reliant mom. And their mom needed those women who helped guide her and shape her to be the woman they needed.

North Carolina had not proved to be the most devastating experience. I had continued to develop my circle of strong women. That circle consisted of the most amazing female friends that a girl could ever be blessed with: Donna Mitchell, Maria Ewing, Barbara Smith Blackwell, Wanda White, and Penny Russell, to name a few. We have remained friends for the past forty years. We have shared many personal moments: births

of our children, recitals, birthday celebrations, Thanksgiving, and other memorable experiences that will always be cherished. I consider myself blessed, despite going through a rough time. These ladies were my rock!

THERE IS NO PLACE LIKE HOME

It was time for me to leave my North Carolina life in the rearview mirror. Home was not where I thought it was; home was where it always was. With a grade-schooler and toddler in tow, I headed back to D.C. and into the open arms of my family. When I left North Carolina, I didn't look back. I moved on from that relationship. And unfortunately, my soon-to-be-ex had moved on from my children. The most challenging part of my divorce was that I was unable to break the cycle of "broken home" for my children. I would have loved for them to have grown up in a home with a Mom and dad who loved them and each other.

Once I had moved back to D.C. with two small children and no employment prospects, I never felt I had time to mope or get caught up in my own disappointments. I needed a place to live and a job. I was able to find both. A new career awaited me, and I was entering a new phase in my life. I wonder if I hadn't watched my Mom and older sisters pursuing careers and raising children on their own, would I have had the perseverance to strive and succeed? Is it nature or nurture? Perhaps it's a combination.

Every decision I've made, both personally or professionally, was always made in consideration of the impact it would have on my children. They needed to know I was going to be ok because that would mean they were going to be ok. Six years later, I was able to purchase a home for us. I bought a five-bedroom house with a three-car garage by the time I was thirty-seven, in the most affluent African American community in the United States. It was a struggle initially, but I was determined, and my children were great motivators. I was never focused on material things, but I wanted a comfortable life for the three of us. After working so long and for so many hours per day, I felt we deserved to live in a beautiful home. God truly blessed us as a family!

Raising a son and a daughter requires different dynamics. My daughter, Toya, seemed to have moved on from that part of her life that was missing a father.

My son, Billy, still wears the scars of a man he never really had a chance to know with any real father-son affection. That's my one disappointment. I know my children appreciate the love I give them and all that I've done to manage a loving home, with God at the forefront of our lives. I couldn't be a substitute father for them, but I hope to be the best Mother I can be for them, loving them more than any two parents could, enough so they won't ever feel short-changed. I instilled in them the love of a family. My children never missed a birthday or Mother's Day without giving me the most beautiful cards with expressions of love for me. Sometimes, they purchase cards just to say, "I love you." It's the simple things that children remember growing up.

EARNING ONE'S KEEP

I feel incredibly fortunate to have had some fantastic friends in my life. These are people I can't imagine being without. My sister was a T.V. anchor in multiple markets, and she suggested that I talk to people and take a look at a career in radio.

A childhood friend, Joe Gotham, introduced me to one of those people, a man named Lenny Chapman, sales manager of WHUR. With no experience in radio, I decided I wanted to be an account executive at one of the major radio stations in D.C. We sat down and spoke a while about me wanting a career in radio. He told me that I could not start at the "number one" station. My response was, "Yes, I can, and I will!" I bugged him so much that he hired me! It was a blessing, in that, it paved the way for a whole new and exciting career for me.

I worked for several radio groups until I landed a job at V103 in Baltimore, and from there, my career blossomed. I was hired to be the director of a department and to manage the first "For Sisters Only Expo" in 1992. I later moved to CBS Radio- WPGC/Heaven 1580 and produced FSO in Washington, D.C. It was an amazing and exciting job. My children got to meet so many entertainers who were known and some that were young and not yet famous: Alicia Keys, Usher, New Edition, Jada Pinkett, Maya, Danny Glover, Shemar Moore, Kristoff St. John, Susan Taylor, Halle Berry, and many, many more. My children's friends thought their Mom was the "bomb", going backstage to get autographs, and to just be in the mix was so memorable for them. They were right there with me for the entire eight years that I produced the event. I have so many write-ups in papers about the event.

I was interviewed on several local television stations. The money was excellent, and the job was fascinating, but with very long hours of work. I worked for several other Radio Groups, including National Public Radio, until I retired my career in radio. I spent more than thirty years as a Media Executive. It was quite an adventure. I believe a strong, confident, successful, and qualified black woman is an asset to all and a threat to many. Along the way, I've had my share of challenges that forced me to stand my ground. I'm happy to say that I never had to compromise my integrity. I have no regrets on that front.

While being a media marketing executive may have been my profession, there was another calling that really spoke to the person I am. My sister, who worked in disability advocacy, suggested I reach out to an executive of NAMI (National Alliance on Mental Illness). That meeting and everything that followed was prodigious. I connected with the local NAMI chapter, took classes, learned as much as I could, and now I am a trainer, speaker, and fundraiser on behalf of NAMI and people with mental disabilities. It's one of the most rewarding experiences of my life.

I ventured into real estate investing and decided I would get my Real Estate license to learn more about the business. I have been a licensed realtor in Washington, D.C., and Maryland for the past thirteen years and have enjoyed helping my clients purchase new homes and others who have sold their homes. I also spend time substitute teaching. I could never have imagined doing this twenty to thirty years ago. Now that I have more time for me, it seems I want to use much of that time for other people. Life has never been more rewarding from a nonmaterial perspective. I am so much richer because of the lives I've touched and those who've touched me in return.

RUMINATIONS

I'm very grateful to have a wonderful, loving family and to also have friends in my life who have been there through my ups and downs for more than half my life, as I have through theirs. These friendships had endured when marriage didn't. I appreciate these relationships and treasure them more than I can say. Friends are family. I don't ever think these bonds can be broken.

One of those friends was Lenny Chapman. Lenny became my best male friend and was like a dad to me. He always kept me on my toes, both professionally and personally. When his health began to fail, we still continued our insightful conversations as I strolled beside his wheelchair in the mall. He was an amazing friend and father-surrogate.

I'm also very grateful to my Sorors. I've been a member of Alpha Kappa Alpha, Inc. for forty-one years, the oldest Greek-letter organization established by college-educated women. My Sorors are phenomenal. I'm so proud of what we've accomplished for our communities, and especially how we've been a major force on behalf of NAMI. Still, in so many other areas, Alpha Kappa Alpha, Inc. has been on the forefront. These women fill my tank, and I am so blessed to be able to serve and help others. It comes naturally to me! It all stems back to the way I was raised and the village who never gave up on me, or my sister.

I am currently active in a Graduate chapter, Iota Gamma Omega. I am currently the Co-Chair of the Women's Health & Wellness Committee, where the initiative gives me the joy I receive in raising community awareness of critical issues impacting African American women.

LIVING MY MOST OPTIMISTIC LIFE

Reaching my sixties was a turning point for me. It meant not having to work as hard for a paycheck since both my children were grown. My life is on a different trajectory, but to my kids, I'm still as energetic as ever. Standing still is just not me. My sister has described me as a light that everyone seeks to shine on them. I'd like to consider myself more of a lighthouse, using my beacon as a guide to safe harbor. My lifestyle plays a major role in helping me to maintain my senses and to stay sharp! When people ask me my age, their response is usually, "No way! You look great at sixty!" I smile and say, "You will, too." It's often younger people. I am not boasting about myself. I am blessed beyond measure, and now I can really show young peopl how a real grown woman can enjoy her life in her sixties. It's not like when our Moms were in their sixties. Or perhaps, we were just not paying attention.

Being in your sixties means a limitless life. It means not holding your tongue if you don't want to, but it also means not wasting your time on anyone, or thing, that doesn't merit all you have to offer. I've lived through the Civil Rights Movement and saw a black man elected President. I've been alive long enough to know that every generation has its struggles and requires sacrifice and service. Now, more than ever, I want to be part of the solution to all of the problems I see around me. Experience has taught me why it's so important to never stop being engaged.

We all change physically, in some measure, as we grow older. The difference between growing older and growing old is that you embrace growing older and accept growing old.

I have no control over getting older, only how I use this part of my life now. For me, it's still about being the best mother, woman, sister, daughter, aunt, and friend I can be. Sure, I've slowed down a bit. I don't have the body of a twenty-year-old, but I love my body!

But here's what a lot of younger people don't know about what's ahead for them: We never stop loving or needing love. Age doesn't render us incapable of desiring intimacy. And life is remarkably funny! I think I laugh more than I've ever laughed in my life. But life is also tragic and mysterious, and lovely, and meaningful. It's everything! And you need to be strong to survive it. We earn every wrinkle and grey hair like a badge of honor. They don't mean an end to anything. They mean we've just been on an amazing adventure longer than most, and some may never see. And it's a one-of-a-kind thrill ride, and it's a blessing.

I'm thankful for every day, and I remain optimistic about what tomorrow will bring!

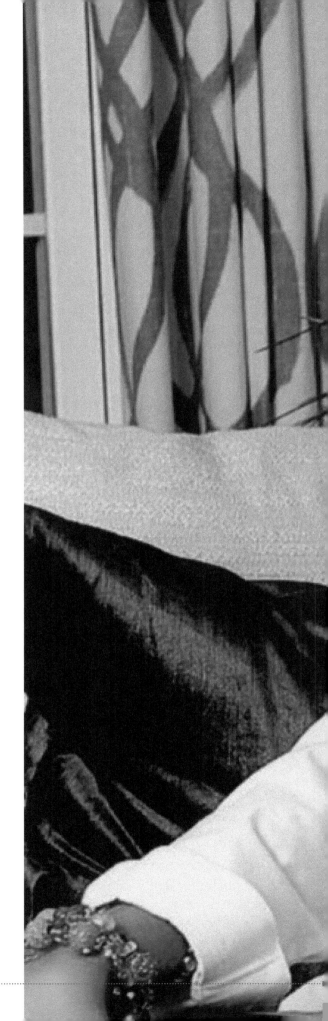

Debbie Morris is a Media Savvy Senior Management Executive with a 32-year career highlighted by rapid advancement and consistent achievement in revenue and profit within extremely competitive markets. Debbie has outstanding qualifications in securing six-figure sponsorships with Fortune 1000 Companies. She has worked for the top-ranking radio stations in the Washington DC metro area including WHUR-Howard University, CBS Radio, Radio One, and most recently WAMU National Public Radio, the #1 station in Washington, DC, where she served as the National Sales Manager. While serving as Director of Event/Sponsorship sales, Debbie also built a successful real estate career in Residential and Commercial sales. She has become an award-winning Associate Broker with Long and Foster Real Estate, breaking many sales records in her region.

Debbie has always been passionate about the well-being of Women of Color and their families. In 1992, she was one of the Visionary women who launched the very first "For Sisters Only" Conference in Atlanta, GA, Baltimore, MD, and later in Washington, DC. Under her leadership, the revenue soared year to year making it one of the most successful events, with over 200 participating sponsors and other local, regional, and national companies.

Debbie has served as a certified instructor (Family to Family Class) for the National Alliance of Mental Illness (NAMI). She was recognized and presented many awards, including one from the Honorable Ben Cardin, United States Senate for her outstanding work in NAMI.

Debbie is a native Washingtonian who was raised in a close-knit extended family. She has two children. She received her BS degree from Fayetteville State University and did graduate studies at University of Maryland in Business Management. She is an active member of Alpha Kappa Sorority, Inc. and currently serves on the Executive Board and as the Co-Chairman of the Women's Health and Wellness Committee.

Florence Champagne, 61

UNDERSTANDING PURPOSE THROUGH PAIN

Florence Champagne

When God gives you a call, a purpose, a mission, a desire deep down inside your heart, what do you do? How do you respond? Well, in my younger years, I felt that I needed to understand exactly how something was going to work out and how it would be done before I stepped out there to do anything. I needed to see and understand the details about everything in advance.

The questions that came to my mind were:

- How will it all come together?
- How will I get the money for that?
- How will I continue to pay my bills?
- What is the guarantee that it will work?
- Who is there to help me?
- What if I fail?
- What will everyone think of me?

After trying to come up with the answers, I would ultimately cave in and say, "Never mind, forget it. It's too hard." I had literally talked myself out of it before I ever even got started. I realized that by going back and forth in my mind, I ended up paralyzed to the point of not doing anything at all. Can anyone relate? Therefore, my attitude would be, "I'll just go with the flow," "I'll see what happens." I did what I thought would be acceptable to everyone without looking crazy.

Growing up, I considered my mother the perfect cook and the perfect housewife — she kept our home beautiful and always prepared excellent meals! Mom had everything in place for Dad and the entire family, and she did it all while working a nine-to-five job with six children — all my father had to do was come into the door, sit at the table, and receive his food. The entire time I watched her, soaking it all in, assisting, and learning. It is not hard to see that this reference point was all that I knew; to listen, serve, be quiet, and not cause any trouble. I became good at it. After all, I grew up in an era of "Children should be seen and not heard." If somebody got out of line, someone was going to get a beating.

As I reflect on all of the attributes that I learned, I realize that I was also learning the fear factor. If you messed up, there would be harsh consequences. I discovered that I was never fully becoming myself, or coming into my own, so to speak. In my mind, I felt that having visions and goals were a little far-reaching and unrealistic, especially when I have failed at some things. When you get burned, you don't want to touch that stove again. God had to knock me off of my feet and have every door shut in order for me to pay attention to His calling for my life. So, the answer to the question: "What do you do when God gives you a calling?" I came up with some options:

1. You listen
2. Be forced to listen, or
3. be hard-headed; God only knows where that will lead you.

It wasn't until my forties that I found myself in an "unlearning" process of everything that I had previously learned. I had to shift from a subservient mindset to a "you are worthy" mindset. This took some time and courage for me. As a matter of fact, at sixty-one, I am still learning.

Throughout most of my twenties and thirties, I was making great money as a legal secretary. Working for someone else, sitting down at a nice desk, dressing in business attire every day, receiving instructions on what needed to be done, and collecting a paycheck was good, honest work. I thank God for my years of experience as a legal secretary at a law firm in Philadelphia. I started in what they called a "Secretarial Pool." I was a fast typist — a skill learned from junior high school that stuck with me and paid off. Still, I was conditioned to operate in a subservient role; I even enjoyed getting the leftovers from their meetings.

Following my work in Philadelphia, I went on to work at other prestigious law firms in the city. Then in Washington, D.C., I found that the attorneys were particularly good at giving me instructions; there was both structure and status in this environment. I understood the hierarchy of the firm: the partners' role, the associates' role, the administrators, clients, and paralegals' roles, and the research, litigation process, billable hours, and patent and trademark. Everything was accounted for and billed down to the penny: your time, the copies, the food, etc. This was a culture and environment I loved, and I was eager to serve, get a good paycheck, and receive any leftovers.

When God speaks, He may have to talk a little louder for some people, including myself. I believe that each person is different based on their experiences, perceptions, upbringing, culture, and spiritual temperament or character traits. Being a Christian woman, I learned through my Bible studies that my spiritual temperament is *Melancholy*.

Some traits of Melancholy are being a deep thinker, carrying the weight of the world on his or her shoulders for the sake of doing good to help others, and focusing on the details, not the whole picture. I have always been that way from being a little girl. With that, I tend to have a perfectionistic character trait — either it's perfect, or I don't do it. Yes, I'm a black or white type of person. Don't judge me; I'm still learning and working on myself.

When something is not perfect or when I can't see my way clearly, it gets very depressing for me. That's the melancholy in me. As a visual, when I paint, I paint exactly what I see. If it's not perfect, I would become paralyzed and not complete it. Take my magnolia painting, for example. It was important for me to show the reflection of the light bouncing off from each leaf. I call this trait both a blessing and a curse. It's hard for me to be an abstract artist because I can't see it; therefore, to work on myself, I paint what I don't see. That's what I call working towards the middle. Like in my painting, "Pieces of my Heart," this is my attempt at creating what I don't see. Even with that, I still have to have that structure — do you see what it is?

Right! I could have either left it alone stages ago and let the viewer use their imagination, or I could lure your eye in to see exactly what it is.

This piece was vital for me to figure it out as I went along, doing it afraid. Woe is me. I would think, why would God want to use me—a person constantly vacillating about the best option for others to see what I'm trying to say. I thought to myself, I'm not even worthy of being used by God. I can trace my spiritual temperament to Moses' biblical character, who was also a "melancholy." He was depressed and doubted himself, but God used him anyway, so I am in good company.

I have found that to get your attention, God may speak in unexpected ways; such as "You're fired," or you may be forced to close your business, the stock market crashes, or you find yourself on the floor while having a heart attack, stroke, or other debilitating illness.

You feel like the rug was pulled out from underneath you, and boom, you hit the floor, or you're in the hospital, or you're unemployed or have a sudden death of a loved one. Could this really be God speaking in an unexpected way?

Do not get me wrong, I am not saying that God caused it, but God allowed it. So, I ask you the question, "When you can't do anything, then what? You have no money; you have nowhere to go. Heck, you can barely breathe; what do you do about your calling? I tell you, the one thing I know for sure is that when you are down in the valley, all you can do is be still and surrender. I'm not talking about in a "How did I get here" kind of way, but in a "Yes Lord, I'm listening" kind of way. That is when you can truly surrender and answer God's call.

Fast forward, in my fifties, I found myself unemployed and uninsured. I was secretly becoming discouraged and depressed. I say "secretly" because, as Christians, some could be very critical, and you could be judged for having a lack of faith if we dare use the word "depressed".

So, giving up, lacking faith, or being depressed was something that I had to keep to myself. I was taking a women's Bible study class at church. In class, I listened to praise reports from other women giving their testimonies. Someone was sharing what God had done for them, and in my mind, the words became "blah, blah, blah." I know she was saying something important, but I said to myself, "When am I going to have a testimony? When are things going to change for me?" A few days later, I had a heart attack at the age of fifty-three, which required emergency open-heart surgery. Be careful what you ask for.

During my recovery, I could not help but think of Job in the Bible. Job lost everything he had: his family, wealth, and was even struck with disease and boils all over his body. But the part of Job's story I felt more connected to at that time, was when his wife said to him, "…why don't you curse God and die?" (Job 2:9). To be honest about it all, I have also felt like cursing God and dying. I was ready to throw in the towel, but I was still here. I survived. I looked around at all of the problems that I had, and cried out to the Lord — while holding my chest — "Why did you save me? Why didn't you just let me die!?" Then, I heard that still, small voice say, "To tell your story."

I was shaken. At that moment, I just began to cry out, "Yes, Lord. Yes, Lord. Yes, Lord."Now, I had a mission . . . *to tell my story.* God gave me a new purpose through my pain.

While lying flat on my back in the operating room unconscious, God sent an angel, my cardiologist, who fought for my life. While I was recovering, it was God who saw to it that all of my bills were paid, when I had absolutely no means of income. God surrounded me with His angels, bringing me food, money, bathing me, cleaning my house, you name it. As I look back, I truly felt that it must have been manna from heaven - you don't know where it's coming from, but it's all taken care of.

While recovering, I had a vision of going before the Lord, and Him saying to me, "What did you do with the talents that I gave you?"

I thought about the parable in the Bible, in Matthew 25:14-30, about the talents and gifts. I recalled the story of how some servants invested their talents, doubled them, showed it to the Lord, who said, "Well done, thy good and faithful servant. You have been faithful over a little; I will set you over much." However, there was one servant who buried his talent. He was afraid to use it for fear that something would happen to it.

There's that word again — "fear."

Therefore, the Lord took away the one talent and gave it to those who had doubled theirs. That servant was considered worthless.For the first time, I felt the sense of urgency to do what God told me to do because now I know, firsthand, that tomorrow is not promised. I wanted to use my gifts and talents while I still had time. Therefore, as I laid in bed while recovering, I completed my first book, "Inez's Granddaughter". I took all of the twenty years' worth of journaling and pouring my heart out that I had accumulated over the years and finished my first book. I did not want to die; then, to go before the Lord, not having one thing to show what I have done with my gifts and talents. Again, I finally found purpose through my pain.

At the age of sixty-one, I feel that I am a late bloomer. In other words, I truly have not begun to come into my own until after the age of fifty.

Through my recovery process, God began to pave the pathway for me. He opened doors for me that I could not have ever opened on my own. I began to speak all over about my near-death experience, my experience with disparities in treatment, my symptoms, challenges with the health insurance system because of having no insurance; you name it. All I know is that God told me to tell it, so I told it all.

I was approached by an organization called WomenHeart, the National Coalition of Women with Heart Disease. I became one of their champions and a National Spokesperson. I was able to speak on

Capitol Hill, the Dr. Oz Show, do educational videos, at health forums, write articles, and even more.Heart disease is the number one killer in the United States. Not only that, but African American Women and Women of Color are also disproportionately affected, and I was one of them. Even though I was being educated, speaking, sharing my story, writing articles, leading groups, being on panel discussions, I felt that there was a part of my experience being left out, a part of my soul and spirit that was not being ministered to, the part about the struggles and disparities in treatment in trying to get help.

I realized that there was a gap between the haves and the have nots; a gap between being able to have good health coverage, being taken seriously, and getting medical attention. To address my experiences and those who looked like me is when I founded the Open My Heart Foundation. Our mission is to help eliminate heart-health disparities among African American Women and Women of Color. I spoke for someone else for a few years, and then I began speaking for myself. We received our 501(c)3 status in 2015, and we celebrated our fifth anniversary as a nonprofit in 2020.

God is not finished with me yet. I am still a work in progress — with even greater things to achieve. The one thing I know to be true is that the older I get, the less I worry, especially after God showed me what He could do for me as I lay flat on my back. Some of the things I have learned along the way are:

- It's never too late. It doesn't matter what the age, just do it. Tomorrow is not promised. If you fail, so what, you will fall forward and closer to your vision.
- God will give you what you need when you need it.
- Learn to trust and believe.
- Be yourself. Don't try to be someone else.
- Don't be afraid to switch up and go in another direction. It's okay . . . you don't have to be perfect, and you don't have to know everything in advance.
- Take the time to hone your skills so you will be ready for your time.
- Don't be afraid to put yourself out there.
- Stay curious.
- Learn to love yourself. Be intentional. Stop looking for others to validate you.
- Take steps in the direction you want to go in. Do it afraid and do it blindly. God will open the doors.
- When one door shuts, God will open another one.
- Be open to receiving it when He does.
- Be happy with the timing of your success.
- Trust the process.
- Don't wait until you are at the end of your life to start fulfilling your dreams.

I want to end by quoting some sage advice that I recently learned from supermodel, Jacky O'Shaughnessy, who was discovered by American Apparel while just eating in a restaurant, and who, by the way, did not start her modeling career until her sixties:

> *"When people talk about age appropriate hairstyles,*
> *and age appropriate dressing, well, whose age? And who are you?"*

Why should I have to cut my hair? Beauty is a matter of perception. Every age has its advantages and challenges. Accept where you are now, not ten pounds from now, or once you've done this or that. Love yourself. It's the springboard to everything else.

I look at myself as a late bloomer, as someone who has not come into her own until later in life, so I value each stage of my life: being a young mother and single parent at the age of twenty-one, learning how to live independently in my thirties, becoming a homeowner in my forties, and then having a major heart event in my fifties have all been valuable seasons of my life. I have worked at the White House and the House of Representatives, taught children, had everything, and lost everything — you name it. Nevertheless, they have shaped me and molded me into the person I am today.

In my sixties, I am still learning that it is never too late for God to use you. I'm in a different season now. Late bloomers not only bloom, but they flourish, through good times, bad times, weathering the storms of life into blossoming now, in this season of my life. Remember, God can turn your test into a testimony; He can turn your tragedy into triumph and give you beauty for your ashes, no matter what stage of life that you are in. You are always becoming what God wants you to be. Embrace it all!

*F*lorence Champagne is an accomplished Author, Artist, and Social Worker. Throughout her professional career she has served as the Director of Social Services at nursing homes in the Washington DC area, as well as provided services for youth in DC Public Housing, individuals with mental illnesses, and continues to provide services for the disadvantaged and low-income families throughout the DMV. She has provided constituent services for the United States House of Representatives for Maryland's 4th Congressional District and worked office of legal counsel at the White House during the Clinton Administration.

Florence suffered a heart attack March 2012. She was misdiagnosed several times before she had emergency open heart surgery. Being a heart survivor, she shares her testimony and personal story of survival and disparity. She found purpose in her pain as she provides support, advocacy, and leadership to women who are either living with or who are at risk of heart disease through the only national organization for women with heart disease called WomenHeart. Through WomenHeart, she has had the opportunity to be on the Dr. Oz show, write heart health articles, appear in educational videos, and speak at heart health events throughout the DMW.

In 2014 she launched her own non-profit called the Open My Heart Foundation. She is a published author, publishing her first book called, "Inez's Granddaughter". Look out for her second book, "Understanding Purpose Through Pain" soon to be released, where she openly discusses the effects of stress and depression on the heart, as well as the risk factors of cultural influences, family history and lifestyle. She is from Philadelphia and resides in Upper Marlboro, MD. Through her many gifts, she enjoys expressing herself through her writings and through the arts, as she aims to heal the hurting.

Gloria Wilson Shelton, Esquire, 66

THE JOURNEY OF AWAKENING

Gloria Wilson Shelton, Esquire.

It is not easy to write about one's self, especially when trying to decide what to share and what not to share. There were many starts and stops along the way for this writer. But I finally decided that whatever I shared for this book and my chapter should be *truth* and ultimately inspire others to continue to live and dream after crossing over obstacles, experiencing disappointments, and encountering unexpected astonishments. This is a story about my journey, or at least a piece of it, over the past sixty-plus years and my eventual awakening.

THE JOURNEY OF AWAKENING

My journey did not have a traditional beginning, nor do I expect it to have a traditional end. What I do expect in the remaining years of my life is to have a continuous journey that speaks to the heart and soul of who I have become, in my awakening to new experiences this God-given life has brought my way. What I desire most is to have the dash between my birthdate and the end date of my life read simply like this: I was a person who dreamed big, was never afraid to take a chance and was excited to explore the unknown, who found the time to reach back to help those who were disenfranchised, and ultimately, found a way to help others achieve their dreams.

Life is full of challenges and possibilities. Some are predictable, and others are not. Who would have thought that in 2020, the world would be faced with a pandemic never seen before; our way of socialization would be forever changed - sheltered in place, wearing masks, schools closed and churches holding worship services virtually? As I reflect on these times, I think about my early years and my best years that have given rise to what I will describe as a newfound awakening to live my best life to the end.

THE JOURNEY OF MY BEGINNING

When I was a little girl growing up in New York, I knew, without a doubt, that I was loved by my mother, father, and sister. They encouraged me to go to college because that was my dream. We were a family of four, nestled in a comfortable three-bedroom house on a tree-lined street in Jamaica, Queens, where most of my fondest childhood memories remain. My mother was my rock, my everything. She was always there for me. She was very stylish and classy and made sure that my sister and I were dressed fashionably alongside her, wherever she went — church, especially, and on Easter and Mother's Day. She had a fascination for coats, dresses, and hats, which I modeled after her.

Our home was immaculate, and every meal was a feast meticulously prepared with an abundance of love by my mother every day. But, not just for our household, but for the entire Wilson-Ellison family tree. Our home was where many family members gathered for Sunday dinners after church, holidays and special occasions, and even often stayed that way for a while after moving to New York from other parts of the South. There was always room for one more, including my cousin, a popular gospel quartet singer, and the members of his group, as they passed through on their various traveling singing tours. My mother also opened our home to care for children awaiting adoption because she felt every child should be loved. From this sprang forth an extended family of brothers and sisters that I still hold close and dear to this day.

NEW YORK TO MARYLAND

I always felt a sense of love while growing up because I was taught values and principles of caring for others, believing in God, and valuing myself as a young lady. Being the youngest child and considered very smart, I got most of the attention. Getting good grades and graduating, almost at the top of my high school class, was part of the motivation that inspired me to go to college. I eventually left New York, my hometown, and settled my roots in Maryland. I must admit that leaving home for the first time was scary. I had no idea what to expect, but I remember thinking I would be lonely, but I didn't realize that my mother would miss me so much more. My sister had already left home, as she married at a young age and was living in Denver, Colorado; so, when I left, our home became an empty nest. So off I went. I attended Morgan State University, one of the best decisions I ever made.

Going to a historically black institution would establish a legacy of memories and relationships of a lifetime, including my membership into Delta Sigma Theta Sorority, Incorporated. However, although it wasn't always clear what I would do once I received my college degree, I eventually figured that out after exploring a few career paths along the way.

AN AMAZING CAREER OF SUCCESS AND DISAPPOINTMENT

My career path is a perfect example; no matter your age or condition, you can succeed. I initially started on the path to becoming a counselor in psychology. But when it was all said and done, I became a litigation attorney, my passion for life! Others saw strength and power within me that I had not — the power of advocacy. The moral of this story is that each path taken, offered this dreamer something different, but always provided an opportunity to renew and create an oasis wherever that path took me.

I became a lawyer after working in the judicial system for several years. I was not your traditional law student. I worked during the day and attended classes at night and on weekends. It was not easy staying focused after studying all night and working a full day job. I was older than most students, but I had a

determined spirit to get my law degree; I finished six months early. Even more impressive, I was afforded an opportunity to serve as a Judicial Law Clerk on the Court of Appeals of Maryland, a coveted position only offered to the brightest law students serving on the Law Review and top ten percent of their law school class. Of course, I was neither. The Honorable Harry A. Cole, Jr., now deceased, afforded me that prestigious opportunity, simply because I asked him to give me a chance. Judge Cole was the first African American judge to be appointed to the Court of Appeals, and he saw in me the tenacity to work hard to prove that I could do it. This experience led to an early offer to work at one of the most prestigious law firms in Baltimore.

Even with these early successes and a chance to make a big salary while working for a large law firm, I decided that I was more of a public servant, leaving a considerable salary behind and entering public service, where I have remained for the past twenty-seven years. What I wasn't prepared for, but endured nonetheless, was the blatant discrimination and barriers an African American woman in a prominently white-dominated profession would encounter years while practicing law. As an Associate with the law firm, I recall sitting in a judge's chambers in Prince George's County and told to be quiet because he wasn't talking to me when I was presenting the position of my client, a major insurance carrier at a prehearing conference. I had a right to speak, a right to advocate at that moment, whether he was talking to me or not because it was the right moment for me to speak on behalf of my client. Yet, this judge would not recognize me in my capacity as a lawyer. Perhaps it was more because I was a woman.

It didn't matter if it was my sex or color. I was a duly licensed attorney accorded the right to defend in that court of law. I went on to serve as President of the Alliance of Black Women Attorneys of Maryland, an opportunity when I found a purpose to share with other young black women lawyers, to stand up and be recognized, but most importantly, respected in the legal profession.

I have appreciated many successes over the years, personally and professionally, but I have also experienced disappointment in my career. In 2010, President Barak Obama nominated me to serve as an appellate judge on the United States Court of Appeals for Veterans Claims. An unexpected surprise, but I aspired to become a judge in my career. I remember receiving the call from the White House, congratulating me on my nomination. How excited I was. I shared the news with my closest confidants, understanding that I still had to clear the majority Republican Senate and House Veterans Affairs Committee to get to a confirmation hearing. I solicited the help of my mentor and godfather, a former federal judge, who was so proud of my nomination, to figure out next steps. I received calls from my alma mater, friends, and colleagues from everywhere, congratulating me — which was overwhelming. I was reminded that since this court had never had a black woman nominee, I would be a first.

Over the next few months, I would realize that politics takes no prisoners. When my nomination was to move forward for confirmation before the Senate, I received a phone call from the White House, informing me that a Senator had derailed my nomination. The process is such that if one person in committee votes against you, your nomination does not move forward. I was heartbroken and devastated. I thought this was the end of my career, my lifelong dream to become a judge. Why? I shortly realized that it wasn't the end for me. It just hurt like heck. Eventually, I had to move on following that devastating experience, which I did.

Since then, I have continued to thrive and flourish in my career. Something inside of me refuses to give up, despite unfortunate circumstances. I am still standing, still achieving, and embracing my best life at sixty plus.

BE PREPARED FOR THE UNEXPECTED

A lot has happened since that moment following my Obama nomination. A few years later, I was faced with an unexpected event in my marriage. I was served with divorce papers after being married for over twenty-five years, another unexpected event that left me filled with disappointment and heartbreak. I wish I could explain what happened that brought my marriage to an abrupt end, filled with domestic violence and painful memories, but we discussed a reason. What I do know is this — weeping may endure for many a night, blaming yourself will end, anger will eventually leave your heart and mind, and joy will ultimately come.

There are lessons to be learned, no matter what your age or condition. Life did not prepare me for domestic violence. It happened in other households, but never to happen in mine and certainly not to me. After all, I was a professional woman, an attorney, in the perfect marriage, living large. And then, one day, all of that changed. There was no more love, and all I was left with for years was embarrassment over what happened to me, regret that I didn't get out sooner, and debt. I never thought, as I did at the time of my nomination to the U. S. Court of Appeals for Veterans Claims, that I would be able to get out of bed and back up on my feet, to return to being the passionate person who always smiled, lived each day to its fullest, embraced the beauty of the trees and flowers in bloom, and laugh again to fill the deep hole left in my heart; most importantly, to be able to feel God's loving presence surrounding me again.

Truth is, God never left me during this entire ordeal. The hurt was too deep to feel anything.

ALL THINGS ARE POSSIBLE

The good news is that our dreams are renewable through faith and prayer. It is because of my faith and belief in God that I found purpose and reason to rise and believe that all things are possible. In the midst of still struggling through the divorce and finding myself, I was still thriving in my career. In 2018, I was selected into an executive leadership program. I believe I was destined to participate in this program for all the right reasons. As part of this program, I was paired with a Senior Executive to serve as a mentor and coach. Although I had an opportunity to review several resumes of these executives as potential mentors, I didn't find any who stood out that I could connect with. At the time, my focus was to select someone who had a mutual interest in the law.

Several highly regarded individuals in the program recommended that I speak with a certain executive who was also highly regarded. It was curious to me why it was always the same person being recommended to me. However, I didn't give it much thought until the Director of the program paired me with that person anyway. Instead of embracing this pairing, I felt the opposite — this was not going to be good. But God knows the plans He has for us if we just step out of the way and let Him do His best work. This mentor reached out to me, scheduled a time to meet, and seemed relentless on helping me, more so than I was about receiving his help. He eventually got my attention and respect.

After reading my resume and working with me for several months, he told me that he found me impressive, smart, and too good for what I thought I wanted to achieve in the last chapter of my career. I began to trust him and felt he would be honest with me. He saw in me untapped possibilities and shared his thoughts with me about that. In him, I saw someone who, I felt, genuinely cared about me and was willing to help me reach my goal. He was becoming much more than my mentor, in an unassuming way, but not as a lover. As graduation was approaching, he shared with me that he had recently lost his wife. Saddened to hear this, I realized that during his time of loss, he had been there for me. He never missed a meeting, always found time to take my calls, review my documents to achieve perfection, prepare me for job interviews, and even coach me through so many of my insecurities.

Anything is possible if you believe the best can happen for you in any situation or circumstance. My mentor told me to never give up on my aspirations, and in return, I told him to never give up on me. He would later realize that I was worth the time and effort he had invested.

HAPPINESS RESTORED

During this experience, another unexpected surprise event occurred. After my divorce, I did not give up on life, but I did give up on finding love again. I worked through the pain and blame, but deep down inside felt an emptiness, a longing to have a partner, but fearful the right person for me did not exist. I was not one to try the popular online dating craze. I wanted to meet my knight in shining armor that would rescue me and make me smile and laugh again. I didn't know when, where, or how this would happen, if at all, but I asked God that if it was His will, to send the right someone to me.

After my graduation, my mentor and I promised to stay in touch. It seemed as though it was too soon to cut the cord of our relationship and the close bond that had surprisingly, but appropriately, formed between us. Unknown to me at the time, he had feelings for me but did not want to compromise the professional side of our relationship, so he kept his feelings on the hidden until he felt it was right to introduce me to that side of him. Truth is, for me, I just wanted to remain friends. We stayed in touch, mostly by email, to check in now and then. We always promised to meet for dinner or something in between, which neither of us ever really

pushed to happen. I was quite comfortable with the occasional emails to say hello and had no personal interest beyond that point in our relationship.

And then it happened. A year later, I found myself having daily conversations with my mentor, coach, and now friend. All of this time, he never let on his feelings for me, until we saw each other for what we call, now, our first date. There doesn't seem to have been an in-between to this story . . . just that our friendship has developed into something special that only four words can describe: *"My cup runneth over."* While this is all fresh and new for both of us, I never thought I would find anyone who could make me smile and laugh again. This is not a love story; it's too soon to put that label on it. However, I can genuinely say that, right now, this person makes me feel categorically *Sexy*, *Classy*, and *Badass-y* at sixty plus!

MY AWAKENING: MY CUP RUNNETH OVER

This is a story about my journey from my early years, career challenges I experienced, how I overcome hurt and pain, and how I am now awakening to find unexpected surprises and a new purpose that I am starting to embrace. Some of my dreams have been fulfilled along my journey, while some remain unfulfilled; however, I am waiting to see other possibilities. I am optimistic that no matter our age or condition, there remains time and hope for us to embrace the unknown and limitless possibilities that lie within us if we give ourselves a chance. What I know for sure is that I now realize a new zest for life; something new and exciting has awakened within me, and I am living each day to welcome in the next one as the best years of my life!

Gloria **Wilson Shelton** is a resident of Anne Arundel County, Maryland. She received her Juris Doctorate Degree from the University of Baltimore School of Law and holds a Bachelor of Science in Psychology and a Master of Science in Criminal Justice Administration. She is a certified mediator in Alternative Dispute Resolution, and a graduate of the Asian American Government Executives Network SES Development Program, Federal Executive Institute Leadership Program (FEI), Leadership Maryland, and Leadership Anne Arundel County.

Gloria currently serves as Deputy Chief Counsel in the Office of General Counsel at the U.S. Department of Veterans Affairs where she serves as primary legal advisor to the Secretary on employment, labor, and EEO law and litigation matters. She has served in the Office of the Attorney General of Maryland as Chief Counsel for the Maryland Automobile Insurance Fund, Principal Counsel of the Courts and Judicial Affairs Division, and as Assistant Attorney General for the Maryland Department of Corrections. Additionally, she was appointed Deputy Legal Counsel for the Baltimore City Police Department and worked as an Associate at Semmes Bowen and Semmes. Gloria had the honor to also serve as a Judicial Law Clerk for the Honorable Harry A. Cole on the Court of Appeals of Maryland.

Gloria has been elected and appointed to numerous national, state and local positions throughout her illustrious career. She was elected as the first African American woman to Chair the ABA Judicial Division Lawyers Conference, and the first lawyer appointed to Chair of the ABA Judicial Division Standing Committee on Diversity in the Judiciary. She has served as President of the Federal Bar Association (Maryland Chapter) and President, Alliance of Black Women Attorneys of Maryland. Her public and community service involvement includes; Golden Life Member, Delta Sigma Theta Sorority, Incoporated, The Links, Incorporated, National Coalition of 100 Black Women, Board of Directors, Boys and Girls Club of Anne Arundel County and Annapolis, Board of Directors, Baltimore Washington Medical Center, and Board of Directors, Girl Scouts of Central Maryland. Gloria has been honored twice as one of Maryland's 100 Top Women.

Peggy A. Morris, 69

BEAUTIFUL MEMORIES NEVER DIE

Peggy A. Morris

As I took a break from the bombardment of the daily news surrounding this thing called Coronavirus (COVID-19) — a pandemic that has already killed more than one hundred and seventy--five thousand people right here in the United States alone — and the protests surrounding "Black Lives Matter" injustices, I've taken a moment to realize how truly blessed I am. My journey over the past sixty-plus years has been amazing, for I'm sure there have been many opportunities for it to have taken a U-turn for the worse! Hopefully, you will agree, no one could have predicted what life would be like in 2020, for it has been a year like no other!

Hopefully, the older we get, one would realize how blessed they are; and for me, my life journey up to now, in a nutshell, has been full of gratitude. I have been fortunate enough to spend my years growing up with six wonderful and supportive siblings, a pair of loving parents who always instilled in us, no matter what, "We stick together"! I have attended elementary, middle, and high school and made it through college. Not to say that there were no stumbling blocks along the way, but I made it through!Such as being a single parent, giving birth to my son, Aaron,who is one of my life's greatest joys and I'm so proud to say, was born on Martin Luther King, Jr.'s birthday, January 15.

With that alone, I'm honored to say that this life has been a true blessing! Being able to return to Morgan State University to complete my education and maneuver my way into mainstream corporate America, nonprofit, and county government throughout my forty-five-year career, the loss of my Dad, marrying my best friend, having the opportunity to travel outside of the country, including Ghana, West Africa, using my gift as a photographer to capture some fantastic moments, building incredible relationships with the many beautiful people who have crossed my path, and to have been blessed to be connected with so many influential individuals has added value to my life's journey.

As I sit here day by day, into my fifth year of retirement, I have invested my time wisely during this uncertainty to continue to grow, build relationships, collaborate with others and restructure my baby, Sisters 4 Sisters Network, Inc. (which I'll elaborate on further), all behind closed doors for even with this pandemic, I cannot stop now! It's so amazing how much you can accomplish when you can sit still and stay focused!

It's amazing how things happen in life that cause you to do something that makes a difference in your life and others' lives.

I often get asked what made me start an organization with women in mind, like the 'Sisterhood' that I have built. My response has been that I grew up with five wonderful and supportive sisters, and when I moved from Baltimore to Prince George's County, MD, to begin my career in corporate America, I noticed that women who looked like me did not celebrate each other. We were not rallying around each other in support, nor recognizing the beauty within. So, I decided that if I ever got the opportunity, I wanted to create a platform where women could come together to allow us to "toot our own horns," celebrate each other, and to recognize their self-worth to help elevate each other to accomplish their dreams — and guess what? I did!

I am blessed to have five beautiful and supportive sister friends:Clara, Yvette, Marlene, Michelle, and Cheryl, who I did bond with in corporate America. Today, some thirty years later, we are still connected in a supportive and loving way!

This is what you call true Sisterhood!

This experience motivated me to create a women's organization with three beautiful sisters (hence the number four):Sharon J. Bullock, Dee Adams, and my cousin, Audrey Dickson. In June 2002, Sisters 4 Sisters Network, Inc. was born, now a 501C3 nonprofit organization. Our slogan is "Women Helping Women to Connect," and we have connected hundreds of like-minded women over eighteen years, using our four core pillars:

- Domestic Violence
- Education & Mentoring
- Entrepreneurship
- Health & Wellness

We have also added another platform to get our message out, loud and clear, a web tv show called *4 Sisters Live!* It is broadcast every Saturday and can be viewed online or via FaceBook Live and on YouTube .

As I continue to reflect, I remember over eighteen thousand employees lost their jobs during the telecommunications downsize, and I was one of them. Lucky for me, I had twenty-three years of service, when so many had no tenure. I was able to walk away to seek a new career opportunity, and it afforded me to explore my passions.

I remember one hot summer evening, a group of friends and I got together to attend a basketball game at the MCI Center , when Michael Jordan was with the Washington Wizards. I was not really into basketball, but went for fun and friendship. I recall sitting there, eating a hot dog with nothing but mustard on it. While everyone else was enjoying the game, I pulled out a pen and began to write two of the things that I was most passionate about on my napkin. On one side, I wrote that I wanted to build a photography business, and on the other side of the napkin, I wrote that I wanted to develop and expand an organization for women.

My friends, who noticed that I was not really into the game, turned around and asked what I was doing. I told them that I was writing down my dreams, and they laughed at me. My response was, "Well, Michael Jordan got his, and it is time for me to get mine!" I walked away from that game with my own game plan to make it happen. The next time we met, I had moved forward and built my photography business and co-founded Sisters 4 Sisters Network, Inc. So, my lesson learned was, "Just Do It!" Go for your dream — plan and take action!

Due to COVID-19, I have now been allowed the opportunity to sit for a moment to reflect on one main lady in my life: my paternal grandmother. She truly inspired me to love photography, and although stern, she was one strong and powerful woman who encouraged me to live life to the fullest! As I watched her work hard, I noted that she also played hard. She loved cooking for others and taking pictures with family during the holidays. And guess who her assistant was? Me!

When I visited her, she pulled out tons of photo albums, and we sat around the kitchen table for hours, as she described every soul in detail. As I went through tons of photo albums that my grandmother left behind, I noticed that there were very few pictures of me, and after thinking about it, it explains why, because my grandmother made me the family photographer.

Whenever we traveled to Virginia to attend our family reunions, it was my responsibility to oversee the camera. Now that explains my passion for photography, for it was already in my DNA!

As I continue to reflect, I feel my grandmother's spirit in my space, as if she were checking on me to ensure that I had possession of her numerous heirlooms and photo albums that had been collected over many years. She had the best of the best in collectibles, as well! I have so many wonderful memories of my grandmother as a child. I'm so thankful to have been blessed to have a few moments to think on on the many rewarding life experiences that I can truly cherish for a lifetime — especially for being the oldest of the grandkids. Hence, you know who the favorite was!

She was a loving woman who worked very hard to support her family when my grandfather passed. She never thought to remarry until over thirty years after his death. I recalled, my grandmother worked as a seamstress at a high-end department store in Towson, MD, during which time she had to enter the store via the back entrance. She worked tireless days and nights to provide for her family. I recall my grandmother would go to work in a green uniform that she got the best wear out of, but come Sunday morning, she had the biggest, most gorgeous hat and the sharpest suit on that any woman would love to have. She was always dressed and ready to go to church. I didn't always like church, but she made sure that I showed up with my camera by my side.

As my love for photography grew, my grandmother ensured that I was at every family reunion and family holiday celebration. She would come and get me the night before so she would make certain that I did not have any excuses not to be there for Easter, Thanksgiving and Christmas, to take the family photos.

Now you truly understand where my love and passion come from in photographing family and friends. It's from my grandmother. Now, with COVID-19 in our midst, I have the opportunity to review the tons and tons of photos that I have had the pleasure to take over the years. As I began to pull out my pictures of those individuals who have impacted my life that are long gone, it puts a big smile on my face, remembering the wonderful times with them. When my grandmother passed in 1995, she was eighty-six years old and had lived her best life. She always traveled to the Caribbean Islands, Hawaii, and Canada, which were her favorites, and our family reunion in Virginia. As we prepared to close down her home after her passing, I found many more unseen photos, and guess what? Yes, there were still very few of me. But I knew then, my grandmother had set me up to carry on the legacy of our family. It's a beautiful thing to allow photos to tell your family history.

Thanks to my grandmother, who shared so many stories of our family history through photographs, when I acquired her photos, I now had the responsibility to continue the legacy of telling our ancestral journey.

MY REAL JOURNEY BEGINS

In 1977, my last year at Morgan State University (MSU), I needed five credits to complete graduation, so I took three credits in photography and two credits in broadcasting. My grandmother was still alive, so I went to her home and photographed her as she prepared family dinner. We had the best conversations around family and friends.

After graduation from MSU, I experienced something that I have never been able to explain. I do not know how you would label it, but it was a spiritual push, that I felt was from God, to visit my mother's sister, who lived in Flatbush, New York. If you know anything about New York, you do not travel there alone, just on impulse. Well, I did! For some strange reason, I felt safe and in good hands. On the spur of the moment, I showed up at my aunt's house. She was surprised just as much as I was!

Growing up, I knew that something tragic had happened in my family; it was something my family did not talk about. There was always a dark cloud every time my mother's side of the family got together for an adult folks' conversation. As I grew to begin to understand, I heard bits and pieces of conversations, but still could not put my hands on it. Then the chatter began to be clear, as I grew older, to understand.

I found out that my oldest brother and cousin both drowned behind the house where we lived in Baltimore County, in a little area known as Turner Station. At this time, , I also found out that my maternal grandparents were killed in an automobile accident when a streetcar in Turner Station struck their car.

The conversations had became stronger as I grew older, but no one wanted to talk about it. I asked my aunt to explain what happened to Larry, my oldest brother, and my cousin, Debbie. The look on her face brought back so many memories for her that she left the room and came back with a plastic bag, holding the Baltimore Afro American Newspaper still intact. If you know anything about the Afro, it was and still is today, the oldest newspaper in the Baltimore, Maryland black community.

As I took the newspaper out of the plastic bag, my aunt reminded me that I could not have it, for she had kept this momento for all of these years. When I opened to read it, the headline, dated February 14, 1953, read: "Tots Drown in River"and included a picture of my brother, Larry, and my cousin, Debbie, who had wandered away from the house and were later found in the Patapsco

River, which ran behind our house. As I proceeded to open the paper, there was a picture of me sitting on my mother's lap, along with her sister and her son, Timothy. After all of those years, our family did not talk about it. I did not even know that it was in the newspaper, and to have photographs of the neighborhood kids looking for them both just blew me away.

I also found out that my grandmother and grandfather on my mother's side were killed in that car accident only six months before the tragedy. Unbelievable! Now I understood why the family did not talk about these heartwrenching events . . . because there was so much pain, losing two little ones and our matriarch and patriarch. But now I knew..

I was immediately inspired again by the power of photography, and as a result of this experience, I became more involved in photojournalism. From that moment, I was determined to document as much as possible, through pictures of my family and friends, because photography tells a story. Now you know why I have been so passionate about photography.If you have been in my space, I'm sure I have a photograph of you!

A PICTURE IS WORTH A THOUSAND WORDS

So, let me get back to determining my next plan of action once we return to some level of 'normalcy'. My good friend, Karen Douyon, posted this on Facebook in July 2020, and I would like to leave it with you:

> *Never regret a day in your life;*
> *Good days give happiness,*
> *Bad days give experience,*
> *Worst days give lessons,*
> *And best days*
> *Give memories.*

Remember, beautiful memories will never die! It's time to get back to what I love to do — and that is to enjoy life to the end!

*I*f you know Peggy Morris, then you know her true love and passion for Sisterhood. A native of Baltimore, Maryland, Peggy received her Bachelor of Arts in Sociology from Morgan State University. Her professional career spans over 30 years in the telecommunications industry, 18 years in the non-profit arena and 8 years in county government. In 2015, Peggy retired from the Prince George's County Government in the Office of Community Relations.

Peggy grew up with five sisters and their parents always encouraged them that no matter what, they stick together and today, that sisterly bond is perpetuated through Sisters 4 Sisters Network, Inc. (S4SN). As Founder and President of S4SN, in 2002, Peggy, along with her cousin, Audrey Dickson and two friends, Sharon Bullock and Dee Adams saw a need to create a platform to allow like-minded women to come together to exchange information, resources and contacts to encourage each other to push forward to follow their dreams. This unique organization is dedicated to helping women to build lasting relationships through the art of networking. The organization's focus is Entrepreneurship, Domestic Violence, Health & Wellness, and Education & Mentoring.

Peggy's other love is photography and she takes great pride in her work with 'Still and Event Photography'. She has captured some of the most exquisite photos at conferences, workshops, networking events and celebrations.

Peggy has received many community service awards for her true commitment in helping to make a difference in her community. Her many accolades include: Power Networker of the Year - Phenomenal Woman 2019; Purse, Pump and Power Network - I Declare Greatness Award 2019; 2019 Voice for the Voiceless Award - SpeakerCon; Essence of Sisterhood - Women Who Care Ministries; Men Aiming Higher Community Partner Award 2014; Certificate of Recognition-Women of Prince George's County 2016; Prince George's Chamber of Commerce - Business of the Year; Black Capital Awards - WDC Trailblazer Award; Women Empowerment Conference Leadership Award; Class Act Productions Honor.

Tina Lorné Hall, 60

My L.I.F.E.
(Living Insightfully For Eternity)

Tina Lorné Hall

My name is Tina Lorné Hall.

However, when I introduce myself to people, I anecdotally say that Peace is really my middle name. Maybe it is more than anecdotal; it is actually the foundation of my existence. I am the righteousness of God. I am who God says that I am. I am peaceful. I speak peace in my life; I speak it into existence. I walk in peace. I talk in peace. I only have peaceful conversations. Peace is all around me. I embrace the peace of the Lord. The peaceful presence of God is totally in my mindset. I am positive. I am strong. I am compassionate.

I am loving. I am a visionary. I am focused. I am driven. I am results-oriented. I am surrounded by God's love, mercy, grace, and favor. I do not need written, daily affirmations to motivate me. I am a daily walking affirmation, guided by all that is within me. Since I have shared this much with you, why not continue. Let me tell you a story, but not just any story. I am going to take you through a partial journey called My **L.I.F.E.** (**L**iving **I**nsightfully **F**or **E**ternity). I created this acronym because each of these words speaks to me. **L** – **L**iving in fear is not living at all: **I**-**I**nsightfully, I know that those who believe achieve: **F**-"**F**or I know the plans I have for you;" **E**-**E**ternity is in the moment.

Throughout this journey, you will find scriptures, love, but mostly peace because, as I stated in my introduction: PEACE *is* my middle name.

> *"And the peace of God, which passeth all understanding,*
> *shall keep your hearts and minds through Christ Jesus."*
> *-Philippians 4:7*

It is fitting that the story should start with this Scripture since it was one of my Mother's favorites. Thinking about her makes me think of family. A family foundation is essential. My parents were married for fifty-six years. They had known each other since they were both fourteen years old. To this union, three children were born. My Dad called my siblings and me the *three Ts: Tina, Toni & Terry*. I was born in Winston-Salem, North Carolina, in the sixties. We soon relocated to Baltimore, Maryland. Both my parents were educators, so consequently, I developed a love for education. I was a very shy and quiet child, and even though it was the turbulent sixties for many, not for us. We were raised Catholic, and that was reflected in our schooling. If you know anything about Catholic school or have ever heard anything about it, it is all true. We were raised with a high level of respect for older people, which was reflected in my relationships with my grandmothers, who were a delightful blend of laughter, caring deeds, incredible stories, and, most of all, love. I was very close to my grandmothers, and a lot of who I am today, I owe to them.

My maternal grandfather and grandmother were entrepreneurs, owning a bus company. The transport companies, such as bus lines, were an essential means of transportation during this time in history. My grandmother was also very religious and very strong in her spiritual walk as a Baptist. Remember, we were raised Catholic. Baptists believe in baptism by immersion after being born again.

Baptists believe that the bread and wine are symbols of the body of Christ. As Catholics, we believed in purgatory. Baptists do not. Catholics do not believe in the all-sufficiency of Christ's blood in salvation. Catholics believe that you need to confess your sins to a priest. Baptists confess their sins directly to God with Jesus Christ as an intermediary. You can imagine my confusion as a child.

If that were not enough, my paternal grandmother was also an entrepreneur. She owned a hair salon. We all know how black women feel about their hair. During my youth, the Motown culture brought black music to the forefront and the style and culture of the women of that era, such as the Supremes.Many women wanted to copy the hairstyles of the singers, and others wanted the protest fro of Angela Davis.

Needless to say, whatever look you desired, my grandmother and her staff could provide it. To add to the confusion of my childhood, this grandmother was a staunch Methodist. I just learned about the difference in one, now there is another! Oh my! Catholics have seven sacraments, while Methodists have only two: baptism and communion. Catholics and Methodists hold a few core beliefs in common, such as a belief in the Trinity and the death and resurrection of Jesus Christ. The Methodist Church allows for divorce and does not prohibit members of its congregation to receive the sacraments. The Catholic Church holds that once two people are married, a bond exists between them that can't be severed by any civil or ecclesiastical authority.

Despite their respective religions, whenever I was around either one of these women, I felt safe. Hence, the peace beyond all understanding. A grandparent's love feels like no other. When I am asked who inspires me the most, I respond, "My grandmothers." These are the women that I admire, the women who taught me how to live, and love.

> *"Wisdom is the principal thing; therefore, get wisdom;*
> *and with all thy getting, get understanding."*
> *-Proverbs 4:7*

It can be no wonder, with the solid background that I had, education played a big part in my life. I was raised humble enough to know that I am no better than anybody but also raised to be wise enough to know that I am different from most. Hence, the reason that I entered the University of Maryland, Baltimore County, with a major in broadcast communications. With a bachelor's degree, I hoped to gain the wisdom and skills necessary for an entry-level job — either on-air or behind the scenes at a radio or television station. I wanted more than anything to be an on-air news reporter or to have my own show on cable news.

The old folks always say, be careful what you ask for. I learned that the University, as a commitment to community service and educational enrichment, offered a limited number of highly sought-after *unpaid* internships. I had the opportunity to intern at WJX-TV in Baltimore as the News Assignment Desk Assistant and Production Assistant. I also had an internship in the Mayor's Office of Telecommunications, Baltimore, as a Communications Assistant. In addition, I interned at Cable-TV, Baltimore, as a News Reporter. But did you hear me say unpaid? Where do they do that? I come from a family of entrepreneurs. I have no understanding of the concept of working for free. I understood that the student interns would experience all phases of a major market television station's day-to-day operations, as a supplement to their academic curriculum. But for free? You must know, that got old quickly. With all of my wisdom, there was no understanding there.

"Be still and know that I am God."
-Psalm 46:10

I learned a long time ago, with all of the amazing spiritual women in my life, that sometimes to hear God's voice, you must turn down the world's volume. We often miss hearing God's voice simply because we aren't paying attention. I needed some peace and quiet so that God and I could figure out this career thing. I had just the answer.

Each year, my father shut down work and ran a summer camp program at Camp Glyndon at Lions Camp Merrick, which is supported by the American Diabetes Association. For eight weeks, the camp consumed his life and that of the entire family, especially my brother, who suffered from diabetes. The children participated in outdoor activities: such as canoeing, a challenge course, archery, fishing, nature walks, swimming, storytelling by the campfire, basketball, baseball/softball, and various arts and crafts. What a beautiful place to get away, and as a camp counselor, I was exposed to the outdoors. Our family stayed in the bunkhouses and enjoyed joining the children around the campfires, singing camp songs. Hopefully, for me, close enough to hear God. I had always been an outdoors person, so this was actually more relaxing than work. My father had a saying, "No health, no wealth," which he used when he wanted to emphasize the benefits of the outdoors. If you could think of anything better, the moon and the stars would do that for you.

That experience and others led me to be involved with youth hostels in Europe. Hosteling is the best way to meet lots of interesting people from all over the world. You are surrounded by like-minded travelers who share your love for adventure and your passion for having fun. Unfortunately, hostels are uncommon in the U.S., so many Americans are clueless about them. The one I chose was a mission outreach project.

Through my trek to Europe, I visited several hostels. I traveled to places such as London, Paris, and Germany. It was still enough to experience that sacred echo — the moment where God speaks the same message again and again to your heart. God's plan is always the best. Sometimes the process is painful and hard. But you have to remember that when God is silent, He is doing something for you.

> *"I can do all things through Christ, which strengthens me."*
> *-Philippians 4:13*

A career path is rarely a path at all. The most exciting life is usually a crooked, winding path of missteps, good fortune, and vigorous work. It is almost always a clumsy balance between the things you try to make happen and those things that happen to you. Obviously, I do not have time to tell you about all of the various career paths that I have trodden down. However, I will share the one that gave me the most joy. People always have said, "Choose a job you love, and you will never work a day in your life." Well, they were partially right. I did figure out what I loved, but I had to work at it. However, it never seemed like work at all, and maybe that is what they meant.

For a while, I found myself in Atlanta, or as they say, ATL. There, I fell in love with the company Soft Sheen. Today, it is known as Soft Sheen-Carson, but back in the day, it was just Soft Sheen.

Their mission was to help people of color celebrate their unique, highly individual looks and styles through their line of innovative products, specially designed for them. I was fascinated with the fact that women of color could celebrate their beauty with both confidence and flair. With Soft Sheen and Mizani, the hair care market was a whole new game. Remember, I grew up in a family servicing the black community when it comes to women's hair. Because of this, I recognized the need for high-quality performing products to service the unmet need of Black salons, stylists, and consumers. Armed with this knowledge and my background, I soon had my own distributorship, which I called Lorné Enterprise, where I pioneered an exclusive line of hair care products in the Baltimore/Washington region. A distributor is someone who buys products from suppliers, warehouses them, then sells them to retailers or end-use customers. I absolutely loved going to all of the hair salons and shops in the DMV (Delaware, Maryland, Virginia) area. As they said, it was not a job because I loved what I was doing. My days were filled. I loved the smell of coffee and hair products in the morning, and I floated the streets of my northeast territory as if I were Madam C. J. Walker herself. My motto was 'Happy Hair, Happy Life.' Every woman knows that a gorgeous hair day is the best revenge, for whatever! I felt as Scripture says, that I could do all things.

> *"For we walk by faith, not by sight."*
> *-2 Corinthians 5:7*

Usually, in a story, this is where the conclusion would go; however, for me, this is only the beginning of a new chapter. Now that I have reached my sexy sixties, I have learned a thing or two. First, I have learned to live my life and forget my age. As the old folks say, "it ain't nothing but a number." But I also know that there is much more to learn. First, let me tell you what I *really* learned, and then I will share with you where I am going in this next chapter.

The older I get, the more I realize the value of privacy, of cultivating your circle, and only letting certain people in. You can be open, honest, and real while still understanding that not everyone deserves a seat at the table of your life. The best day of your life is the one during which you decide that your life is your own. No apologies or excuses. No one to lean on, rely on, or blame. This incredible journey is a gift, and you alone are responsible for the quality of it. Open the book of your life only to a few people, because in this world, very few people care to understand the chapters; others are just curious to know or being noisy. I thank God for blessing me with the Precious Gift of twenty-four hours a day. I want to use the rest of my time on Earth wisely. My Dad used to say often, "Time waits for no one."

I have always believed, but now I have learned to welcome the fact that life is to be lived, not just watched. I want everyone to experience life. **L*ive...Live...Live,*** and embrace yourself first, with God. Take the time to enjoy life with others, surround yourself with positive people, and create as many memories as you can.

SMILE... LAUGH... SHARE... LISTEN... LEARN... EXPLORE... TAKE RISKS... PRAY... TAKE ONE DAY AT A TIME... TRULY LIVE

As I turn the life page of sixty, what is in the next chapter? I am ready for this new chapter of this new adventure! The one thing that I do know, for sure, is that the life in front of me is far more important than the life behind me. One of the first projects that I am working on, with my sister, is a legacy project about my mother and her boarding school. I am also working on a book project, which is a book of inspiration. From my own experiences, I know that you are never too old to set another goal or to dream a new dream. I want people to feel my positive energy in this new book of inspiration. My philanthropic goals include my work on the board of CYEYC (Cody Young Empowerment Youth Charities). I have chosen gun violence as the cause to spend my time, my money, and my energy to support. We will never get a serious grip on gun violence in this country until we adopt comprehensive measures to keep guns away from those who should not have them.

As part of who I have *always* been, network marketing still holds a place dear to me. I would like my title in this new chapter of my life to be:

Visionary Consultant/Entrepreneurial Broker

Also, in this new chapter, I want an intimate personal relationship with Jesus encamped with prayer, peace, and mediation, which will strengthen me mentally, physically, and spiritually. To this end, I also see myself as an evangelist. This is right in line with my education. An evangelist is like a newscaster on television, except that the evangelist's mission is to preach God's Word: Simply and clearly telling people what God says and what He has done for all. I must be about this with urgency at this chapter in my life because the souls of people are at stake. Considering that evangelism is a mission, I would like to conduct this work on mission trips overseas. This would be a great revisit to my time in Europe. Now, I would be going on a more critical mission to execute my evangelism plan.

Love is a word that I want to define this chapter in my life. I want to spread the love of God. I want to win over the world with love. Love is the greatest gift that God has given us. To love *life* is to love God. I want to be so busy loving God, loving others, and loving life that I have no time for regret, worry, fear, or drama. I want everyone to know that each sunrise proclaims God's love for us. What I want people to know, by my actions, is that the most significant achievement for anyone is to love God, love yourself, and love others.

Peace, an inner quality, is mentioned four hundred and twenty times in the King James Version of the Bible. I am living my life so that during my legacy, people will know PEACE and be able to say that

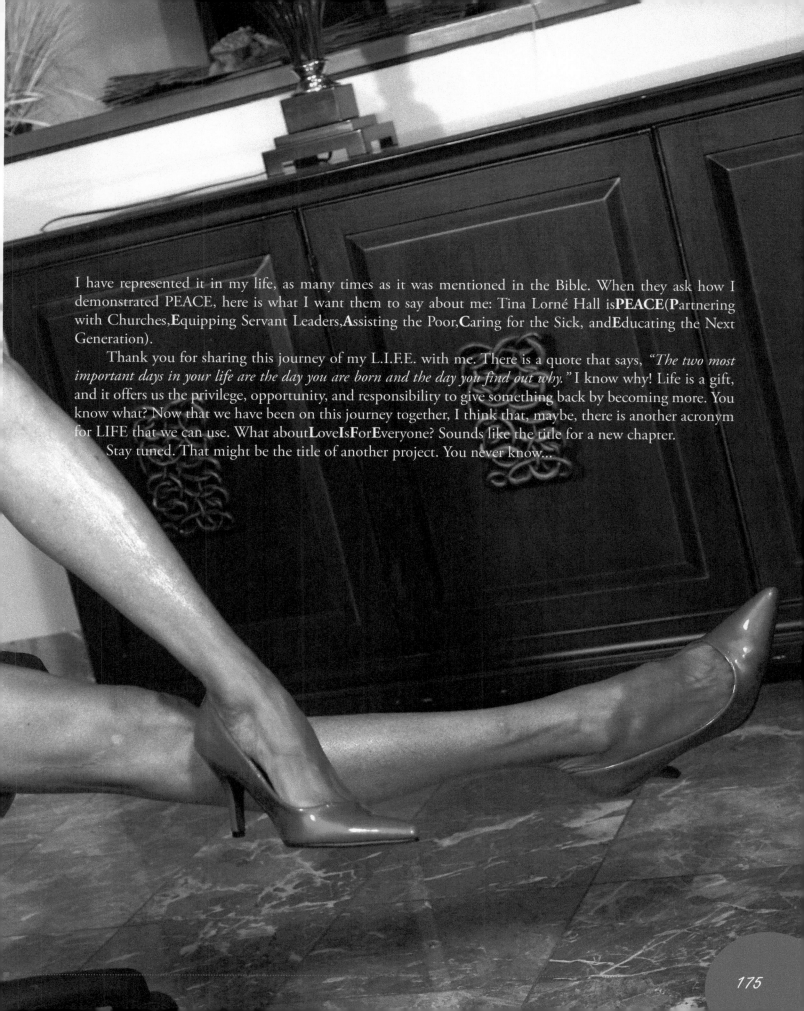

I have represented it in my life, as many times as it was mentioned in the Bible. When they ask how I demonstrated PEACE, here is what I want them to say about me: Tina Lorné Hall is **PEACE** (**P**artnering with Churches, **E**quipping Servant Leaders, **A**ssisting the Poor, **C**aring for the Sick, and **E**ducating the Next Generation).

Thank you for sharing this journey of my L.I.F.E. with me. There is a quote that says, *"The two most important days in your life are the day you are born and the day you find out why."* I know why! Life is a gift, and it offers us the privilege, opportunity, and responsibility to give something back by becoming more. You know what? Now that we have been on this journey together, I think that, maybe, there is another acronym for LIFE that we can use. What about **L**ove **I**s **F**or **E**veryone? Sounds like the title for a new chapter.

Stay tuned. That might be the title of another project. You never know...

*T*ina Lorné Hall is the owner of Lorné Enterprize, a multifaceted organization with a focus on digital marketing utilizing artificial intelligence. In this capacity, Hall is responsible for developing, implementing, and managing marketing campaigns that promote a company, its products, and services. Her customer base is varied and includes health, and nutritional products focused on weight maintenance as well as pharmaceutical sales. Additionally, Hall has recruited, trained, and developed a team with a client that dealt with dental, vision, and prescription plans.

Believing in multiple streams of income, Hall is also a Real Estate/Funding Broker as well as a Health and Wellness Consultant. To give back to the community that gave so much to her, Hall also acts as a Substitute Teacher in the Baltimore City Public School system. Previously, Hall was a Counselor at the Maryland State Department of Education Gifted and Talented Program. Not one to have her entrepreneurial skills levied to one country, Hall acts as a Correspondent Writer for U.S. Express, Tokyo Japan, where she writes about trends that develop in the U.S. for a Japanese newsletter publication.

Hall has put her degree in Broadcast Communications from the University of Maryland Baltimore County to good use in her network ventures. A member of the Maryland Hispanic Chamber of Commerce, Hall is also an Account Executive with WBGR- Sports/Entertainment Network. The Recording Academy- Member of The Grammy Association can be included in her list of accomplishments.

Her philanthropic work includes CYEYC, Cody Young Empowerment Youth Charities board member and media correspondent. Hall is also a Lector at New All Saints Catholic Church in Baltimore. The organization that ties all of her work together is her Lifetime Memberships in Sisters 4 Sisters Network, Inc; a group focused on women helping women to connect.

Sharon J. Bullock, 66

THE IMBALANCE OF MY MIND, MY BODY, AND MY SOUL

Sharon J. Bullock

As a Black Woman, I was told that I could have it all. But no one told me the cost. No one told me that having it all did not mean that I had to do it all. Women of color sometimes do not know how to slow down. As we grow older, it is evident that there needs to be a balance between all aspects of our lives; mind, body, and soul. Balance is a concept that describes the prototype of splitting one's time and energy between all of these essential aspects of life. The problem with the word balance is that there are no secret answers about how to achieve it. So, having developed a new philosophy, I am not going to beat myself up, trying to achieve perfect balance. Now in my sexy sixties, I accept the imbalance in my life. Journey with me on my imbalance of mind, body, and soul.

MY MIND, MY BUSINESS, MY PASSION

I grew up in the small town of Gainesville, GA. I guess you can say we were an average middle-class family. I was the middle child with one older (Kenny) and one younger brother (Duane). Of course, I was a Daddy's girl, with the kindest sweetest Dad in the world! I can remember growing up, my Mom had great style and was always dressed to the nines from head to toe. She believed in quality, and it was reflected in what she bought for herself and me.

We went to church a lot, and hats were expected. A deeply rooted tradition in the African American community, wearing flamboyant hats to church has both spiritual and cultural significance. It is said that the hats were designed by women to "catch God's eye" in hopes that He would hear their prayers. Culturally, African American women strut with "hattitude" and hats became a part of me in later years. We went shopping in Atlanta, versus in my small hometown because my Mom liked to be *different* from everyone else. I believe that I inherited this from her, which is why I always want to stand out from the crowd and be *different*, too! It also has a lot to do with my shyness. I am an introvert and will seldom be the first to approach others. Sometimes, what I'm wearing causes others to approach me instead. I was also influenced by my Aunt Faye, who had five beauty salons and a Beauty school. I worked in one of her salons as a Receptionist and Shampoo Girl, while I was still in high school. I even bought my first car, a Rambler, during my Junior and Senior years! I wanted to own my own business one day, too. Entrepreneurship was in my blood.

As a pre-teen, I always wanted to be a model. I was intrigued by Black women in the fashion industry. My idol was the top supermodel, Beverly Johnson, and I wanted to be just like her! Johnson rose to fame when she became the first African American model to appear on the cover of Vogue Magazine. I dreamed of being on the cover, and inside magazines, and walking down the runway. Growing up, I attended the Ebony Fashion Fair in Atlanta, and other fashion shows, which were another influence from my Mom and my aunt. I could see myself in this fantasy world. Fashion became my passion! Upon graduating from high school, I was accepted and was going to attend Barbizon School of Modeling. However, as I watched my childhood best friend, Donna, and others pack their trunks to go to four-year colleges, all of a sudden, I felt left behind. I eventually changed my mind and followed my friends instead. I immediately applied to Morris Brown College in Atlanta, fifty miles from home. I later transferred to Morgan State in Baltimore, MD. Morgan became my best years, as I pledged and became a member of Delta Sigma Theta Sorority, Inc., where I still have very dear friends.

Nevertheless, that little girl inside of me still wanted to be a model. I suppressed this feeling by determining that if I can't be a model, then I wanted to look like one! I always had to be the "*Best Dressed*" and would always dress other people in my head, even daydreaming about fashion and clothes, and being on the cover of magazines. No one would ever know this because I didn't want people to think I was conceited or "self-centered". Little did I know, this was indeed my passion coming through.

I majored in Mental Health, and minored in Psychology, because I thought I wanted to be a Child Psychologist, of all things! While working in this field briefly, I took on a part-time job at a women's clothing boutique called *Paraphernalia*. My passion was reignited, and this became my favorite job! Through this part-time job, I met someone (Denise Logan) who introduced me to the hair care industry, which was more geared towards the beauty industry - that helped keep my passion alive. I worked for haircare manufacturers and brokers in the professional and retail fields, in sales and management. After working in my aunt's salon, I was very familiar with the industry and was right at home there. The hair and fashion shows were exciting and led me to pursue entrepreneurship. I wanted to open a Day Spa, but would have many challenges getting it financed. I spent fifteen years in this industry, but also received my makeup artist license and became a certified Color Analyst, as well.

I pursued my own business a few times. I created my own private label makeup line called "Make Me Over", which I sold to my clients at trade shows, home parties, and one-on-one. I even bought into a small computer makeover franchise, which showed women how they would look in different hairstyles and makeup. Still, the east coast wasn't ready for this new craze at the time. After returning to the hair care industry and moving to New York very briefly, I found myself jobless. I went to work in the telecom industry for what was supposed to be a *pit stop* until I got back into the industry I loved. This move lasted another fifteen years instead.

During that time, I still kept the doors open with my passion. I worked part-time as an Image Consultant and freelanced as a Makeup Artist for Fashion Fair, Elizabeth Arden, Shiseido, and Lancôme in department stores. I loved enhancing a woman's beauty and building her self-esteem.

Later, I began making jewelry and selling it on my job and to whoever would buy it! As I shopped for materials to make the jewelry, I discovered it was easier to buy and sell, versus making it myself. I then created *Metamorphosis Jewelry Designs*, which I marketed online, vending at different venues and home shows.

The jewelry became a hit, and I added hats, belts, handbags, and scarves. My clients loved my total look and encouraged me to carry clothes, as well. After a few years, it was too much to move around, so I started looking for a storefront. I mentioned that I wanted to open a Day Spa, which would have a boutique, spa services, a food bar, and a salon. Silver Spring, Maryland, was revamping its downtown, so I approached the landlord with my concept. They loved the idea and offered a lease. However, my silent partner – who was helping me get it financed – and I had a significant disagreement and ended up parting ways. Now, I was on my own and had to approach the landlord alone.

Mind you, I was underfinanced, with little to no collateral, but determined. It didn't work out, so I put the Day Spa on hold. Fast-forward two years . . . I approached them again, with a boutique idea instead. They suggested a location that was too small, so I came back. This time, the space was occupied by a tenant that was leaving soon; it was the ideal location! I didn't look anywhere else. It was perfect! An all brick, corner store with lots of windows, in a busy Whole Foods shopping center. I could imagine my name on the building and my clients coming in. I drove by there every day after work, sat in the parking lot, and stalked the building while visualizing it was already mine. I did this for six months because they didn't tell me no!

Ironically, six months later, I found out that my employer was planning a RIF (Reduction in Force) in my department. I didn't have the building yet, but I asked the Lord for signs. I prayed that if this was for me, I would need three things to happen:

1) the building,
2) a severance package and,
3) ninety days – unheard of during a RIF, which is usually two to four weeks!

One by one, all three fell into place, and I knew this was for me! God had answered my prayers. In November of 2007, with the help of my sisters from "Sisters 4 Sisters Network", I opened my doors as

Metamorphosis Wardrobe & Accessories Boutique. It was an AMAZING store! Just like I dreamed it would be. I had to pinch myself many times, so I could wake up from this dream that came true! I experienced a whirlwind of success for about the first ten months. I had traffic galore, with customers coming from all directions. We had the right merchandise (including hats, clothing, jewelry, handbags, accessories), a full staff, and happy customers. Prior to opening the business, I had all of my contingency plans in order, with five credit lines, significant savings, a severance package, 401K, and excellent credit. But nothing could have prepared me for what happened next.

First, in June 2008, there was a fire at my townhouse. We had just moved into our new dream home in March 2008, which had taken us ten years to build! It was a beautiful contemporary cedar home with glass walls and huge cathedral ceilings that we had custom built. We were preparing our previous townhouse to be rented before the fire. Second, in September, construction began in front of my store for a new civic building and an ice-skating rink, which would last two years! I was the new kid on the block, and now I'm blocked by tarps, causing my flowing traffic to

come to a halt because no one knew I was there unless they had been there before! Third, in October, the infamous 2008 Recession hit! Retailers suffered! And last, but certainly not least, immediately after this, my husband, who was in the car industry, lost his job! Since I had just opened the business, I was not taking a salary, so we depended on my husband's income to cover our household expenses, while I covered the business expenses. The contingencies we had to support the business were not initially put in place for us to live on. But we had no choice.

I began to spiral downward quickly. I had to choose between my business and our beautiful new dream home, but I could not have the home without income. My landlord even offered me a deal, or an out. However, I still had hope, and I had already experienced the good side. I knew what the business COULD do. Plus, I knew that what was COMING with the new civic center and ice-skating rink had the potential to bring even more traffic to my store. What temporarily saved the business was the County had an Impact Fund, for situations when they impacted businesses during construction such as this. I could apply for this grant, which I did, and received the same. In the meantime, I decided to create my own traffic by having fashion shows, book signings, plus In-Store, and Out-of-Store promotions. Two of our best book signings were with Author, Inspirational Speaker, and TV Personality, Iyanla Vanzant. I later became her Stylist for a brief period of time.

Nevertheless, I still had to choose, and my dream home lost that battle. The devastation was overwhelming! The house that took us ten years to build only gave us four years to live. I remember refusing to leave the house the day they literally auctioned it off to the highest bidder, while I watched from an upstairs window, curled up in a fetal position. I still shake when I hear a certain doorbell tone. It takes me back to that feeling of complete helplessness and the tremendous fear I felt, thinking behind that door might be the Sheriff coming to escort us from our home, even though it didn't happen that way. No words can express the humility, the devastation, the sadness and shame during and after a foreclosure. Unless you experience it, you will never know. Thank God we still had the townhouse!

After the recession, it was a tough road back; I was still climbing out of a deep hole – robbing Peter to pay Paul just to stay afloat. Having to live on the funds meant for the business would soon run out. My once perfect credit would go into the toilet. After a seven-year struggle, having to depend on hard money loans, was soon the demise of my business. Although I had another three years with the business after losing our home, both losses still hurt deeply. I remember going into a deep dark depression after closing the doors of my business in December 2014. For days and months, I sat or lay in my room, looking at four walls for hours at a time, barely eating or moving from that one spot. This depression repeated itself a few months later, after losing my best friend from college, Cherie'. The losses together were unbearable!

Somehow, through time and the grace of God, I found the strength to move on. Nevertheless, I would do it all again in a heartbeat because. . . *fashion is still my passion!*

MY BODY, MY TEMPLE, MY LOVE

My body is my temple. For me, that means that I respect my body. I treat it well. I'm happy with the choices I've made in preserving my temple. I never acquired a taste for alcohol, thinking it had a nasty bitter taste, so I don't really drink, except virgin drinks or cranberry and orange juice. When we were very young, my cousins and I almost burned my grandfather's barn down as we hid in the haystacks trying to smoke Kool & Camel cigarettes! I can still remember that pain in my throat when trying to inhale. So glad I didn't inherit that habit either. I don't eat red meat or pork, just fish and poultry — no sodas or sweet drinks, only water at room temperature. My only vice is chocolate!

There is one ritual I swear by and have real testimonies about it below. A Japanese ritual, which a friend (Charlene) forwarded to me from the internet; it truly works, and the health benefits are amazing! I drink thirty-two ounces of water at room temperature on an empty stomach daily when I awaken each day. I then brush my teeth and wait forty-five minutes before I eat or drink anything. Do not drink anything cold after a meal, as it will turn your food into sludge and begin to clog your arteries. Drink soup or hot tea instead. This ritual claims to reverse cancer in six months and Type II Diabetes in thirty days, among other diseases, and all eye diseases, as well (disclaimer: this an opinion only).

A side effect is you will lose weight and maintain the loss if you make it your daily routine. My testimonies are that I had a positive mammogram (a mass on my breasts) and a positive pap smear (polyps on my cervix). After following this routine for five to six months, both tests came back negative! I also had these recurring corneal ulcers from sleeping in my contacts. I've been doing this routine for over two years now and have not had this issue since. By the way, I've lost over seventeen pounds without dieting and have kept it off, just by drinking the water first thing in the morning! Walking and Tai Chi are my favorite forms of exercise.

I am a witness that love can be great when you're starting over at any age. I have been married twice, and have one stepson, Jonathan. The first time, I married my father. Archie was very kind and gentle like Dad. He even looked like him! We grew apart, and it started to feel like a platonic marriage. There was more romance in my second marriage with James. We were together for twenty-seven years. However, things fell apart towards the end. We remained best friends. Six months after we parted, he was diagnosed with pancreatic and liver cancer. Though we weren't physically together, I couldn't and wouldn't let him go through this alone. I stood by him until he took his last breath, almost one year later. He was a gentle giant with a heart of gold, who never met a stranger. I will always miss his wonderful laugh and his compassionate spirit. God prepared me in advance for this devastating loss. He knew I wouldn't have been able to handle this had we still been together after his diagnosis. He never puts more on us than we can handle.

After being married most of my adult life, I didn't have a clue how to date again. Online dating had received a bad rap. I won't swear by it, but I do believe it is another option for meeting the opposite sex. Remember, you are in control! You do the screening, and you make the rules on how and where you meet. If you don't feel any chemistry during the first meet and greet (always in a public place), there is no second date! I admit that it has been challenging to date again. I do believe we must teach men how to treat us. And no, chivalry isn't dead! And yes, I've found love again!It's also true that when we as women reach our sixties, we're at our peak sexually. Another best kept secret is coconut oil, go figure!

I now feel comfortable in my own skin and confident in myself and who I have become – and am still becoming. I have no regrets, and I make no apologies for being me. For the first time in my life, I'm seeing the mature woman as sexy and desirable. I am still evolving and exploring new things; I'm open and honest with my feelings, and I know what I want and what makes me happy, and I won't settle for anything less. I am now a priority, not just an option!

MY SOUL, MY PURPOSE

"To whom much is given, much will be required." (Luke 12:48). If you have heard this, you know that it means we are held responsible for what we have. If we are blessed with talents, wealth, knowledge, time, and the like, it is expected that we benefit others. Now in my sixties, I am still living my passion through fashion and benefiting others as a Wardrobe Coach, Stylist, and Color Analyst. All of us have a purpose in our lives, a reason we were created, a reason we exist. My passion made room for my purpose. I love making women feel beautiful on the outside, so it can permeate on the inside, and make them feel good about themselves, becoming the best they can possibly be, in every sense that matters! Everyone likes getting compliments. There's nothing better that can boost our self-esteem. I use Color Analysis to prove you will ALWAYS look good when you're wearing your "Best Colors". My motto is, "Why look good some of the time. . . when you can look AMAZING All of the time?" My passion for making women look amazing on the outside has now developed into my purpose to make them feel amazing on the inside as well.

That little girl did make it on the runways, even though mostly at the finale of my own shows! She also made it into some magazines, even the cover, although they were local ones. They were right! I can have it all! I just do not have to have it all at once. In my sexy sixties, I realize that only I determine the balance or imbalance of my mind, body, and soul!

Sharon J. Bullock is in her sixties and is living out her best years. Growing up in Gainesville, Georgia, and later moving to Maryland and Washington, DC, Sharon's journey to sixty played an intricate part in her being the visionary author for *Embracing My Sexy Sixties!* 20 Inspirational Stories from Phenomenal, Confident & Beautiful Women.

Sharon is a graduate of Morgan State University and a member of Delta Sigma Theta Sorority, Inc. She is also Co-Founder & Vice President of Sisters 4 Sisters Network, Inc., a non-profit organization that empowers women. She is an Elite member of Entrepreneurs & Professionals Network (EPNET) and Bold, Brave & Beautiful, a member of eWomen Network, Women Business Owners, Circle of Champions, and Women Business Network of America.

Sharon began her career in the hair care industry in 1979, in Sales and Management, for companies such as, M&M Products, Soft Sheen Products, and FML Manufactures Brokers for over fifteen years. She held such positions as, Account Manager, Assistant and District Sales Manager, and National and Regional Merchandising Manager, respectively.

After receiving her make-up artist license through Von Lee in Baltimore, MD she studied to become a Certified Color Analyst, as well. She started her own private label cosmetics line, "Make Me Over" in 1983, and began her part time business as an Image Consultant. She also Freelanced as a Make-Up Artist for companies such as, Fashion Fair, Elizabeth Arden, Lancôme, and Shiseido.

Sharon's range of expertise and knowledge as a Wardrobe Coach & Stylist, Image Consultant, Certified Color Analyst, and a former Freelance Make-Up Artist, as well as her Corporate experience at Verizon for 15 years, has prepared her to walk into many exceptional opportunities. Her passion for Beauty and Fashion launched the opening of Metamorphosis Jewelry Designs and then Metamorphosis Wardrobe & Accessories Boutique in November of 2007, where she served as the Owner and Chief Executive Officer. Sharon is also the former Stylist for world renowned Author, Motivational Speaker, and former Talk Show Host, Iyanla Vanzant.

Sharon is the co-recipient of the 2008 African American Empowerment Weekend (AAEW) Legacy Female Entrepreneurs of the Year award; A 2008 Diamonds Xcel Elite Achievement Award recipient; a 2009 recipient of Gamma Phi Delta, Delta Phi chapter's Economic Development Entrepreneur of the Year Award; 2010 winner of the Top 100 MBEs (Minority Business Enterprises) Award; The 2011 Washington Business Journal Minority Business Leaders Award; A 2011 recipient of the Potomac Valley Alumnae Chapter of Delta Sigma Theta, Inc's, Minerva Entrepreneurship Award; Winner of the Black Capitol Awards II, in Washington, DC, Recipient of the Class Act Community Awards in 20012, and A 2019 Trail Blazer Award Recipient for Be There Magazine.

Sharon's journey to sixty plus encompassed trials and triumphs. Through it all, she learned how to persevere toward her goals, to activate self-love, embrace self-care, and to become the best version of Sharon J. Bullock, in every sense that matters. Sharon quotes, "We are not our mother's 60's. I am Embracing My Sexy Sixties and living out my best life. Who knew it would be this much fun!"

AFTERWORD

Thank you for purchasing and/or reading this book. Sharing these inspiring stories through this journey has been a labor of love. I hope you have enjoyed them and have been inspired, motivated, captivated, and maybe have even heard your own stories throughout these chapters.

I want to thank my **Amazing** Co-Authors for their perseverance, patience, and understanding throughout this whole process in birthing this baby for you and others to read, and most importantly, for trusting me with their truths and giving me the pleasure of sharing their stories with you.

This book is truly for all ages and genders; however, if you are a woman in your sixties or know someone born in this *exciting* decade, please share this book with them and/or join us as a co-author in our next volume of *Embracing My Sexy Sixties!* **20 Inspirational Stories from Phenomenal, Confident & Beautiful Women**. It's time to tell your stories! You can sign up through our website, www.embracingmysexysixties. com, or contact us at info@embracingmysexysixties.com.

We welcome your feedback and look forward to sharing many more stories with you in the future!

Amazingly yours,

Sharon J. Bullock.

Visionary Author

AUTHORS' DIRECTORY

(By Chapters)

1. PAMELA REAVES SCRIBER
Business Name: NELLA, LLC
Email: pamreg01@gmail.com
Facebook: https://facebook.com/Pamnellallc
Instagram: pamelareaves
Twitter: @pamela_reaves
LinkedIn: www.linkedin.com/in/pamela-reaves-a210b831
Website: Pam4NELLALLC.com
Phone: (443) 507-8415

2. CONIECE M. WASHINGTON
Email: coniecewashington@gmail.com
Website: coniecewashington.com

3. DR. CYNTHIA SAMUELS BROWN
Email: Cynthia.browndst@gmail.com
Facebook: Cynthia Brown
Instagram: Ladybeetle10
Twitter: @CynthiaBrownVSU
LinkedIn: Cynthia Brown

4. LAURA L. DORSEY
Business Name: LLD Consulting
Email: laura@lauradorsey.net
Facebook: Laura Dorsey
LinkedIn: Professor Laura Dorsey
Website: https://lauradorsey.net/
Phone: Business (240)714-6966
 Cell (407) 719-0225

5. MAEION BRYANT
Business Name: Maeion Beauty & Co, LLC
Email: Mobilebeauty17@gmailcom
Facebook: Maeion Beauty & Co
Instagram: Maeion_Bryant
LinkedIn: Maeion Bryant
Website: Maeion Bryant Beauty & Co
Phone: (443)360-7371

6. SYLVIA GARRETT
Business Name: 5LINX/OXZGEN
Email: sylvia.scg@gmail.com
Facebook: http://www.facebook.com/sylvia.scg
Instagram: scgsylvia
Twitter: scgsylvia
LinkedIn: Sylvia Garrett
Website: linktr.ee/bestlifelive and www.scg.prosystem101.com

7. SYLVIA HEADEN DOUGLIN
Email: sylvia.douglin@refinedtraining.met
Website: www.refinedtraining.net
LinkedIn: Sylvia Douglin

8. ROSETTA ARINTHA THOMPSON
Business Name: RT Inspired Designs
Email: rtinspireddesigns@gmail.com
Facebook: https://www.facebook.com/rosetta.thompson.98/
Instagram: rainbowrock2
Twitter: https://mobile.twitter.com/CakeLadyZett/
LinkedIn: https://www.linkedin.com/in/rosetta-thompson-8780a817/
Website: www.mydailychoice.com/rathompson
Phone: (410) 979-0792

9. LINDA MARIEA MARSHALL
Business Name: Team Revolution
Email: lindam0210@gmail.com
Facebook: Linda Marshall
website wealthownership.acnibo.com
Phone: (202) 341-6362

10. ANGELA C. GAITHER-SCOTT
Email: acgaitherscott@msn.com
Facebook: Angela Gaither-Scott
Instagram: agaitherscott

11. BETTY ENTZMINGER

Business Name: Just BE Entertrainment
Email address: bettyentzminger@gmail.com
Facebook: facebook.com/JustBe4
Instagram: Bettyentzminger
Twitter: twitter:@bettyentzminger
LinkedIn: linkedin.com/in/Bettyentzminger

12. ANNETTA WILSON

Business Name: Annetta Wilson Media Training and Success Coaching
Email: Operations@SpeakWithEase.com
Facebook: facebook.com/AnnettaWilson1
Instagram: instagram.com/annettawilson12
Twitter: twitter.com/AnnettaWilson
LinkedIn: linkedin.com/in/annettawilson
Website: www.SpeakWithEase.com

13. MIRIAM D. MARTIN, MD

Business Name: MD Medical and Wellness Center
Email: DrMartin@mdmedicalandwellness.com
Facebook: https://www.facebook.com/miriamdmartinmd/
Instagram: https://www.instagram.com/md_medical_and_wellness_center/
Twitter: https://www.twitter.com/FlyWeightDoc
Website: https://mdmedicalandwellness.com/
Phone: (301) 808-0341

14. REV. DR. D. AMINA B. BUTTS

Business Name: The Believe Center for Change, Inc.
Email: drdbutts@msn.com
Facebook: RevdrdAminaButts
Instagram: revdramina
Twitter: Rev. Dr. D. Amina B. Butts
LinkedIn: Rev. Dr. D. Amina B. Butts

15. DEBBIE MORRIS

Business Name: Realtor
Email: debmaria1005@gmail.com
Facebook: Debbie Sparkle Morris
Instagram: Debbie_sparklemorris
Twitter: debsparklegirl
LinkedIn: www.linkedin/debramorris

16. FLORENCE D. CHAMPAGNE

Business Name: Open My Heart Foundation
Email: florencedchampagne@gmail.com
Facebook: https://www.facebook.com/florence.d.champagne
Facebook: https://www.facebook.com/openmyheartfoundation
Twitter: https://twitter.com/DutchChampagne
LinkedIn: www.linkedin.com/in/florencechampagne59
Website: http://openmyheartfoundation.org/
Phone: 240-389-4361

17: GLORIA WILSON SHELTON, ESQUIRE

Email: gloriashelton@mac.com

18. PEGGY A. MORRIS

Business Name: Sisters 4 Sisters Network, Inc.
Facebook: sisters4sistersnetwork.org
Instagram: #S4SN
Twitter: #S4SN
Website: www.sisters4sistersnetwork.org
Phone: (240) 678-0117

19. TINA LORNE' HALL

Email: visionwithamission@yahoo.com
Facebook: Tina Hall
Instagram: tinaonamove
Twitter: tinaonamove
LinkedIn: Tina Hall

20. SHARON J. BULLOCK

Email: sharon@embracingmysexysixties.com
Facebook: www.facebook.com/sharon.j.bullock
Instagram: www.instagram.com/sharonjbullock/
Website: www.embracingmysexysixties.com
LinkedIn: www.linkedin.com/in/sharon-j-bullock -3143b29/

CPSIA information can be obtained
at www.ICGtesting.com
Printed in the USA
LVHW071230201220
674145LV00073B/862